THE TOKYO-VAN NUYS EXPRESS

POEMS BY
RICK LUPERT

TOKYO HAKONE KYOTO HIROSHIMA

THE TOKYO-VAN NUYS EXPRESS

Copyright © 2020 by Rick Lupert
All rights reserved

Ain't Got No Press

Design, Layout, Photography ~ Rick Lupert
Author Photo ~ Addie Lupert

This book is protected under the copyright laws of the United States of America. Any reproduction or other unauthorized use of the material or artwork herein is prohibited without the express written permission of the author except in the case of brief quotations embodied in critical articles and reviews.

First Edition ~ August, 2020

ISBN-13: 978-1-7330278-1-6

Visit the author online at
www.PoetrySuperHighway.com

The time is right to mix sentences with dirt and the sun with punctuation and rain with verbs.

- Richard Brautigan

Tokyo is huge. Something like 15 million people live there, and my estimate is that at any given moment, 14.7 million of them are lost.

- Dave Barry

Since Auschwitz we know what man is capable of. And since Hiroshima we know what is at stake.

- Viktor E. Frankl

Thank you Addie, Richard Brautigan, Ianthe Brautigan, Brendan, Elizabeth, Richard Modiano, Nobuaki Takahashi, that monkey that climbed on my head, and the people of Japan.

For Richard Brautigan who left out all the unnecessary words

and for Addie who is the wellspring of all my words

PRELOGUE

開始

The Tokyo-Van Nuys Express

Brautigan wrote a book called
The Tokyo-Montana Express.
He's not writing books anymore.
Someone had to do this.

Underwokyo

I
It's been a while since I've
had the opportunity to go
on a two-week trip.

I'm going to need
more underwear.

II
Do they even wear underwear
in Japan? There's so much
I don't know.

Tokyo is the largest city in the world.

They have the busiest intersection
and the largest broadcasting tower.
Their Godzillas are twice the size
as our American Godzillas.
Everything in Tokyo is bigger
than the corresponding things
we have in wherever I am from.

A Two-Week Trip Involves A Lot of Laundry

I don't want to run out of clothes in Japan and ask Addie and our son if they'd mind if I was nude when we dropped him off at Jewish summer camp later today?

Shalom Chaverim!
Here's our son.
Take good care of him.

This is the Poem

This is the poem where I tell you about
the knot in my throat when we left our kid
for three weeks amongst strangers who
promised they'd remind him to brush his teeth.

This is the poem where I describe the last hug
where he patted me on the back several times
and, as you probably know, I wasn't able to
tell him anything.

This is the poem where I tell you about
how he yelled at us for reminding him
a third time to write postcards to people
who love him.

This is the poem you may have read before
or written yourself when you've come to
these times where these things happen.
They grow up so fast. They grow up so tall.

The doctor says he might be five foot six
someday, which is taller than any of his
immediate family. We hope it doesn't happen

while we're away. We're going to Japan
to feel like giants. This is the poem where
we go away to Japan, leaving our son
for what seems like a thousand years.

Driving to Tokyo

I
When I picked up the rental car at Burbank Airport
they saw it was a *one-way* and asked where I was going.
Japan I said, and then I would have liked one of them
to say *our cars aren't ocean certified,* but instead
they told me to have a great time. Actually, if I'm
being honest, they didn't do anything but hand me
the paperwork and tell me what space the car was in.
I drove it away to Van Nuys so it could spend the night
in our driveway before it carried us to San Diego
where we boarded the Tokyo-Van Nuys Express.

II
The Tokyo-Van Nuys Express
begins with a drive to San Diego.
As we pass by LAX I ask Addie
if we should stop in and say
Not today bitches! We're going to Japan!
Addie sighs and says *if you must,*
just please keep your pants on.
Actually I'm not sure she said
please.

III
Addie expresses her excitement that
we are flying *the other way* as we have
never flown west from Los Angeles before.
We're flying the other way and some place
will be there because the world is round
she says confirming centuries of ideology
about the shape of our planet.

IV
A sign on the freeway to San Diego
says *Fog Possible.* Oh, San Diego
even your roads are open to all
the possibilities.

SAN

There is a store in the San Diego Airport
with a sign that says *Grab, Pay, and Go*.
I'm glad they added the *pay* as I remember
seeing a store called *Grab and Go*
and that place was a free for all.

Miles

Through all kinds of voodoo and airline miles and an extra check of my passport which has sat dusty in the closet since Ireland, we are ushered into the airline lounge where a complimentary bourbon reminds me of last summer and the cutest macaroons you have ever seen have Addie squealing and the ocean awaits for us to hover over it for hours and hours.

Amenities

I spend the first hour of the flight
marveling at the amenities of the
business class sky cabin.
I have my own entrance and
may have people over later.
The windows electronically tint
at my command. My seat turns into
a bed and, I assume, is powered
by magic. My personal TV screen
is bigger than the ones I grew up with.
I'm wearing the *Japan Airlines* slippers
I've got the *Japan Airlines* noise canceling
head phones wrapped around my head.
There are pillows and chapstick and
a shoehorn for some reason.
And the food menu...Don't get me
started on the *any time I like* menu.
Addie is watching anime in the cabin
next to me. There's a cheese plate
in my future and so many other things.
This is such a long flight. I'll have time
to describe them all.

Plane

I
I watch *Bohemian Rhapsody*
on the plane. Music is so powerful.
I want music to be president.
I want music to be in charge of
everything. All the parades.
Everything.

II
I'm embarrassed at how friendly
and eager to serve the flight attendants are.
If the engines lost power we would
land safely on their smiles alone.

III
A sea of clouds blankets the Pacific
and probably lasts all the way to the
rainy season in Japan.

It's okay.

If I've learned anything from
Miyazaki films, rain is magic
and will have no adverse
affect on me.

Plus I brought an umbrella.

I'm Concerned About The International Date Line

I haven't slept since tomorrow.
The sun hasn't set since
well, I don't remember the last time.
My eyes want to stay open for
all the things that need to be done.
The disembarkation
The luggage collection
The customs declaration
The stop at the *Klook Desk*
At some point I'll need to
put my shoes on.
I'm dreaming of taking them off
in Shinjuku with the most
convincing *Do Not Disturb* sign
you've ever seen hanging from
my hotel door.

Ground is Coming

I
I can see the shores of Japan
from the inflight cockpit view.

On one of these trips unwelcome cargo
was taken to Hiroshima and, prior to that,

before we were part of the *One World Alliance*
they made a surprise visit to Hawaii.

All respects to those events will be paid
before our feet leave the ground again.

II
Four thousand meters until the ground
and still no Godzilla sightings.

III
It says we're over land but
all I can see is clouds and I'm
beginning to suspect that Japan
exists only in dreams.

IV
This point in the descent
is no time to begin practicing
my ninja screams.

V
I report some of my observations
back to Addie and tell her not to worry
as I don't think it's Godzilla season.

VI
A peninsula of Japanese land pops up
through the clouds. The Tokyo-Van Nuys Express
is coming to your town.

His Influence

If I accidentally use the phrase *Tokyo-Montana Express* instead of *Tokyo-Van Nuys Express* later on in this book, it's because of Brautigan's book. Send me an email with the page number and I'll correct in a future edition.

Bus

I
Everything here is in Japanese!!!

II
I'm noticing the architecture on the road
between Narita Airport and Tokyo
Outside of the fact that everything is in Japanese
and they drive on the left side of the road
and the much smaller cars
and the strange looking trees
and all the Japanese people
and all the signs that say "Tokyo" –
Outside of all of that
this could be anywhere.

III
It's very humid here.
I know I know. It's gotten
to the point where we're
talking about the weather.

IV
There are thirteen million people who live in Tokyo.
I've met several of them.

Goodnight

After twenty two hours of travel
The Tokyo-Van Nuys Express has
set up shop in the far east.

I'm no longer able to keep my eyes open
so forgive any misspellings or non-sensibilities.
I'm not even awake enough to

finish this poem.

TOKYO DAY ONE
建築

All That We Miss

We wake up to news of an earthquake in Southern California which is a shame as I wanted to take Jude to his first earthquake, experience the father-son bonding of huddling in a door way, tell him, with my wisest voice, *No, son, don't drop and roll. That's if you're on fire. You want to duck and cover for these.* I suppose this is just another sign of him getting older and finding his own way. The earth shook in Southern California today, and with all my fatherly powers, I couldn't do anything about it.

Pressure

One of the first things Addie tells me this morning
is *they're serious about water pressure here*
(after the news about the earthquake.)
I spend most of our trips assessing the location
for whether or not we could live here.
After taking a shower at the Hilton, Shinjuku
after experiencing the glory they call *water pressure*
we may not use our return tickets.

haiku

*It is the rainy
season in Tokyo* is
all they ever say.

Love

After Addie asks me
to watch out for slices
of lemon at the buffet
I belch, which, based on
my understanding of
Japanese culture,
is the highest declaration
of love one can make
in a breakfast situation.

Caution

I desperately want to hold Addie's hand
as we walk to meet our tour bus, but
we read somewhere that public displays
of affection are not as well received as
the slurping sound you make when you
suck ramen noodles into your mouth.
I don't know what I did to deserve this life
this hotel breakfast, this ability to be
in this place, this nearby hand and its
magnetic pull to my own.

Sunrise

I
Sunrise Tours offers a thousand tours
every day. We're only taking one of them.
Nine hundred ninety nine more items
for the bucket list.

II
The sticker identifying me as a
member of the tour matches the
color of my shirt and is otherwise
an unplanned eye sore on the
presentation of my visible self
on this first day in Tokyo.

III
Like sheep we follow our tour guide
through the lobby of the hotel.
Also like participants in a tour.

IV
Addie's colorful pants
blend in with the bus seat.
I watch her legs disappear
when she sits. Her eyes
though — Everything else
fades away when those two
things are around.

Time Travel

I'm writing you from tomorrow
I message to all my friends
back in yesterday.

Oh Glory

I
When you walk into a bathroom
and the toilet lid senses your presence
and raises before your eyes
presenting a heated seat
you may find you're not sure
if you should worship it
or if it is worshipping you.

II
The river inside the bathroom
at the Goejin Hotel – The bridge
going over it – There's no place
in the world I'd rather pee.

Read This Ten Times Fast

Tokyo, the capital of Japan
means east of Kyoto
or east of the capital
which used to be Kyoto
but is now Tokyo.

On the Bus

I
There are blue signs on the highway
west out of central Tokyo with
pictures of sleeping babies
indicating there are residences nearby
and you should drive quietly.
So those of you who were planning
on coming here and driving around
while screaming your holy hells
out your windows should rethink
your strategy.

II
We drive by a bicycle prison.
I can't imagine what they did
but I hope they learned their lesson.

III
The Japanese style house architecture
reminds me a lot of the houses in the
San Fernando Valley, most of which
we're built shortly after World War II
which makes me wonder if they
secretly won the war, especially
considering the current state of America
and they seem to be doing fine here.

IV
The Cut Chemist Barber Shop.
No relation.

V
A certain percentage of the people
walk the streets wearing surgical masks.
This is normal here and not worth
calling attention to in a poem.

At the Edo-Tokyo Open Air Architectural Museum

I
A woman scrapes weeds away from
spaces between stones. The battle
between architecture and nature rages on.

II
We see the trolley that inspired Miyazaki
The bathhouse that inspired Miyazaki
The printshop that inspired Miyazaki
Tokyo is Miyazaki and Miyazaki
is Tokyo.

III
All these buildings disassembled
brought here and reassembled.
I hope someday they take apart my house
and reassemble it at a place they'll call
the *Lupert Open Air Museum.*

IV
The panda shaped candy in the gift shop
should rightfully be called *pandy*.

V
Dragonflies occupy the air space
between the museum and the parking lot
as one would expect.

VI
You don't tip in Japan which is a shame
because every one I meet — I want to
give them all my money.

The Ghibli Museum

I
I am prepared to not take photos
inside the museum as per Miyazaki's wishes.
The only recording devices allowed
are biological eyes and imagination.

II
You have to be under eighteen
to ride the cat bus which is a travesty
to everything I believe in.

III
I don't know what movie the
soldier on the roof is from
but I'm going to find out and
watch it when I get home so
I can really appreciate my
photos with him.

IV
A man in front of us
describes *inbetweening,*
an animation process
that fills in motion between
still frames unlike drawing
twenty-four individual pictures
for every second.
And then the math
gets fuzzy when
you start to calculate
how many drawings
you have to draw
to make an entire movie.

V
If there was a sequel
to the movie *Totoro*
it should be called
Twotoro.

VI
As best we can tell
the essential tools for
Ghibli animators are
colored pencils and
cigarettes.

VII
Regarding the people
pedaling the giant
fish with wings:
It's the only way to fly.

VIII
The things you can bring
to life with a pencil and
imagination.

IX
I tell Addie to prepare to
dine with ninja tonight.
That's not specifically
related to Ghibli but I
want her to have all the
time she needs. She
says *and then go up to the
observation deck on
top of the government
building* which excites
me because I had
forgotten about that
and she knows how much
I like to go up things.

X
The introduction to
the short film is delivered
entirely in Japanese
which I have no right to
complain about.

Ninja Shinjuku

We are told to remove our shoes
This was shortly after the young man

told us it was ten thousand yen to enter
And then quickly added he was kidding.

They take us to a private room but there's
a camera so we keep our clothes on.

We're in the room alone for a while
but wonder if the ninja are here already –

They're just that good.
We don't know if we're allowed to go to the bathroom.

We've never been in this situation.
Anything can happen.

We eventually do go to the bathroom
and wonder if the ninja show up

when we're gone and feel defeated
by our absence.

The sign telling us the Master Ninja was
coming says *No Shooting.*

They may be referring to photography
but if they knew how I felt about guns

they'd know it wasn't going to be an issue.
I begin to perform my own ninja magic show

after the master ninja leaves which involves
a swirling napkin and Addie demanding

I pick our souvenir ninja jack-of-spades
off the floor.

Addie speaks to the tea
I wish I could drink you

and then bows to it with an
I need to sleep tonight.

Addie wants to go behind the scenes
to see where the chime rings when

we press the button to summon a ninja
to see the monitors where they view

how complete our courses are.
Addie has ninja tendencies

and is ready for an internship
a *ninj-ernship.*

Did you see what I did there?
I'm like a ninja with these words.

People Who Helped Me Today

Tour Guide San
Bus Driver San
Fellow Tourist San
Waiter San
Miyazaki San
Docent San
Cashier San
Concierge San
Waitress San
Ninja San
Addie San

It is not rude to call people
by their professions here
I was told.

haiku

The Tokyo-Van
Nuys express is going to
sleep. Good night Edo.

TOKYO DAY TWO

猿

Morning Buzz

I hear a series of buzzes coming from Addie
and think she might have been a robot
this whole time.

Turns out it was just her Fitbit alarm
waking her up so the Tokyo-Van Nuys Express
can have another day in Japan.

Excerpt from an Electronic Conversation with Jacob Glickman

It's good so far! [Our trip to Japan]
We keep eating and seeing things.
We also have to learn how to use the subway today.
If you've ever looked at a map of the Tokyo subway system,
it may have caused a seizure. So I'm fairly sure
we'll end up in the ocean or the sky.

The breakfast buffet at the Hilton, Shinjuku is the stuff of champions.

I consider you all to be champions
so, by all means, make your way here
and have at it.

The coffee at the breakfast buffet
at the Hilton, Shinjuku, in Tokyo, Japan,
formerly known as Edo

is the sacred beverage of champions.
You already know how I feel about you
and let's all be grateful I caught the

spelling error and we are left with
champions instead of the
French word for *mushrooms*.

Ninjaddie

While I was gazing into my phone to type the previous poem Addie used her new ninja skills to disappear from the table. Either she's getting some more lychees, or the Yakuza have taken her.

Coffee in Japan

I could drink this coffee until
the end of time. It's that good.
But Tokyo's main attractions
are not going to visit themselves
so I'm leaving this coffee pot
until tomorrow when I hope
it remembers my name.

Poem

All the men's bathrooms say
Gentleman on the door and
every time I enter I want to bow
and say *start your engines!*

Brendan

I'm bringing Totoro home.
He wants to live with you.

On the Ginza Line

I
A Japanese-only announcement
live from the conductor begins.
I nod indicating I understand
what is being said is for my benefit.

II
A man next to me is reading a book
in which the Japanese text goes
up and down, as opposed to the
left to right, or even right to left
I'm familiar with. If I were reading
up to down I'd be worried I'd
fall off the page after every line.

III
I hope the Japanese-only announcement
isn't saying our train stop is closed because
of increased Godzilla activity.

IV
A woman leaps out of her seat
after the train has been stopped
for a few seconds. Her destination
a surprise to us all.

Ueno Park

I
In Ueno park a monkey
crawls all over me and
messes up my hair irreparably
for the rest of the day.

In more positive news
A MONKEY CRAWLED ALL
OVER ME TODAY!

II
A samurai festival has broken out
in Ueno park, or possibly it has been
planned for months and it is only
Luperts who have broken out into
a samurai festival in Ueno Park.

In the Japanese National Museum

I
One Hundred Poems by One Hundred Poets
Explained by a Wet Nurse
Sangi no Takamura,
Katsuahika Hokusai, 19th century

Looks a bit like a canoe accident
but the title was so spectacular
I wanted to go with her.

II
The Actor Formerly Known as Michinosuke
Becomes Segawa Roku IV
Utahawa Toyokuni 1807

and he's got the fat red kimono to prove it.

III
Bush Clover at Night
Suzuki Harunobu, 18th century

She brings her
Chinese lantern or
a box of popcorn,
or both.

IV
Child Receiving his first Hakama Trousers
Okumura Masanohu, 18th century

With such a big head you can give away
all the trousers you want.

V
Monkey
6th Century

This monkey has no body
unlike the one that CRAWLED
ALL OVER ME WITH ITS
LITTLE MONKEY BODY!

VI
Tomoku Bosatsu Kyo, Vol. 2 of 3
766

Addie spots the Japanese Torah.
The lines go up and down leaving us
to free fall into Buddhism like
an inevitable change of scenery.

VII
Standing Bishamonten
Keisan, 1271

standing puppy
human face
seems angry
reason unclear

VIII
Waka poetry was an indispensable heart
to the daily lives of couriers.
Imagine if poetry of any kind was
indispensable to all humans living today.

IX
One sign says *Zen and Ink Painting*
which is either a pun or an
accurate description.

X
Gasuko Type Armor
16th Century

His blond peacock-like hair
takes the edge off.

XI
We enter the Japanese swords room
and although I believe that pens are
mightier than swords, it's still pretty cool
to be in a room full of swords.

XII
Johanti Style Helmet
16th-17th Century

Gaze into my peacock headdress
made of swords instead of feathers —
How the east was won.

XIII
Maps off the World and Japan
16th-17th Century

They made North America look like a
screaming sheep sitting on top of Mexico.

XIV
Writing Box
Edo Period, 17th Century

The writing box —
What about the writing box?
I'm a writer. Do I need a box?
Jesus, I've got to get a box.

XV
Slippers are available
to loan, to maintain the
quietness of the gallery
in case you are a
loud walker.

XVI
Seated Priest Gien
8th Century

has cracks in his chest and
super-large ears, possibly
from the centuries of sitting.

XVII
Standing Sekisei Doju
1537

stands opposite the
Seated Priest Gien
in elevated opposition
to the sitting.

XVIII
Standing Dragon King
1316

stands opposite *Seated Shaka Nyorai, 9th Century*
in a sculpted detente that will last
until the end of civilization.

XIX
What does one do with a ritual spatula
Addie wonders as we enter a room full of them.
Make ritual omelets I suggest.

XX
Kannon Riding a Dragon
Sati Chozan, 20th Century

Dragon used to be the only way to travel
until they invented the subway.

Interlude

Addie slurps her soup with proud glee
during our break from looking at ancient
Japanese art. I am brought oolong tea
which, despite my best efforts with
Google Translate, I am told
Oolong can not strong
I add honey and gaze
at Addie's rice.

In the Archaeology Building

I
We enter the Japanese Archaeology Gallery
and view ancient dug up mundane things –
axe heads and other tools
fertility sculptures, bowls, cups
drinking vessels and figurines
bracelets and spearheads
rusty chest plates.
Some day they'll dig up all
the nicknacks I've been burying
in my backyard for fifteen years.
I'm purposefully creating the
archaeology of the future.
Dig up my coffee mug
my remote control
my Dalek figurines
Don't let what I did here
be forgotten.

II
Jar with Double-rimmed Mouth
Haji Earthenware, 3rd Century

Oh jar with double rimmed mouth
from the third century –
my two lips have waited
centuries to sip liquid
from your two rims.

III
Gilt Bronze Shoes
5th-6th Century

Bronze shoes are cool
until you have to wear them
to war and your victory
rusts away.

IV
In the *Gallery of Treasures* we enter
a room full of heads. Addie suggests this
is where Jude could get a replacement in case
his falls off. This is immediately after
she spotted what she called the *Buddhist Thinker*.
Addie's on a roll and heads will roll!

P.S. it was actually a room of masks.
But masks and heads can go a long way together.

V
Konpei
12th Century

The ritual implement used for treating eyes
looks like the best it could do was to poke your eyes out.
Double sided for your convenience!

VI
I saw a saw
an ancient saw.
There's no chance
they'll let me bring
this back on the plane.

Back in the Park

I
All souls get a
monkey to suck on your thumb
and mess up your hair.

II
I want to ask the people leaving
Ueno Zoo if they'd be willing
to describe the pandas for me.
I know they all saw them and
I'd like to make their memories
mine.

III
A sign says they closed the panda exhibit
for the day, so we decided not to enter the zoo
as we have a strict *no pandas no Luperts* policy.

At the National Museum of Western Art

I
Looks like
they haven't
dusted *The Thinker*
in a while.
I think they
should.

II
Spring (Daphne and Chloë)
Jean-Francois Millet, 1865

Might as well be called
a couple of naked kids
feeding baby birds

III
original frame

has no painting
People stare
hoping one
will appear

IV
We rediscover
Van Gough's bedroom in Arles
that we first met in Paris
at the D'Orsay
We should have carpooled.

V
Mr. And Mrs. Édouard Manet
Edgar Degas, 1868-1869

is missing twenty-five percent
of the painting including
Mrs. Manet's face.

VI
Haystacks
Claude Monet, 1885

I want to lay naked in the haystacks
I once wrote in a famous poem by me.
The two people in hats leaning up
against this haystack had different ideas.
Or maybe I'm just looking at it too soon.

VII
Workers in Snow
Edvard Munich, 1919

This is the only painting that gets its own wall
in the Matsukata exhibit. Every painting
deserves its own wall.

VIII
Vampire II
Edvard Munich, 1895-1902

makes me want to seek out
Vampire I and every other
Munsch painting.

IX
Head of a Man
Jean-Auguste-Dominique Ingres

He threw in the neck
and some of the body.
No extra charge.

X
Water Lilies, Reflections of Weeping Willows
Claude Monet, 1916

Most of this painting is missing
Not even a signature
I want to bring Claude back
His eyesight too
Let him finish this one
And make so many more

Poor Tired Addie in Front of Rodin's *Gates of Hell*

Would you like to sit by The Gates of Hell?
You had me at "sit."

Bon

We have three different waiters
at *Bon*, the Buddhist vegetarian restaurant
where we spend two and a half hours –
The woman, the man and the woman
who, we think, was a magical combination
of the first woman and man.
We're dining in a Miyazaki film tonight.
Imagination has gelled together
an unending concoction of vegetables.
The sake bottle is so heavy
an invisible cat watches us dine
doesn't say a thing.

Goodnight, Tokyo

My dreams came true today
while riding the Tokyo-Van Nuys Express –
A monkey climbed on me and
gave me monkey hair.

We dined in a private room
but the staff came and went from the room
like they owned the place.

We walked and walked and saw
Monet and Munsch. Magnets were
purchased that will someday live
on our refrigerator.

We took the subway and
didn't end up in the sky or the sea.
In a couple of days we will dine in the sky.
Tomorrow, which is less than a couple of days,

we will see where the most people ever
cross the street. We will drink with owls.
Maybe me and my monkey hair will be
replaced by me and my owl hair.

I'll have to let you know. I'm writing this
to let you know. I'm writing this as if you
are reading this. Get ready to stop reading.
I am ready to stop writing.

For now.

TOKYO DAY THREE

雨

It is raining in Tokyo today

which no-one wants except for
the plants, and the people with
rain barrels, and the people who
like the rain. I am none of these and
all the things we have planned
will allow the water direct access to us.
There is the shrine which they
put outside, and the cafe where
you drink with owls, which I think
includes a roof, and the place
where *all the people* cross the street
and it is an event enough to go there
just to cross the street. We plan
to be with the robots tonight.
Though we hear whispers
they are flesh and blood.
So perhaps they won't mind
if we show up wet, to hear their noises
and watch their lights.
Rain changes when it reaches the ground.
It becomes water. It may not remember
who it was before. It may not
know what it will be again.
It is raining in Tokyo today.
Not a hard rain, but a present one.
I'm not sure *one* is the right word.
How does one count the rain?

On the way down to breakfast

a Japanese man
is not sure he has arrived
at the correct floor

and before his
hesitant step out of the
elevator, steps

backwards into the
face of a woman who must
be his wife by the

way she accepts the
back of his head into her
face. She holds her cheek

as they walk together
to what we all hope is
their room.

The elevator
speaks to us in Japanese
which is such a treat

as some elevators
won't tell you
a thing.

At Breakfast

I
One of the tea bags is labeled
Professional Tea Bag.
Oh the career options
I never considered.

II
The coffee tastes burnt today
which is better than the
browned waters of our past
but not as good as the
perfect coffees of our
yesterday.

III
Addie is having *Rice Krispies* this morning
and I wonder what they are telling her.
Everything speaks in Japanese.

IV
She is also having a moment with
the lychee fruit. I won't give you
the details as it feels like what is
passing between her and the lychee
should stay between her and the lychee.

V
An Alternative Ending to Part I So You Can Choose the One You Want

One of the tea bags is labeled
Professional Tea Bag.
You can be anything you want
In Japan.

VI
It is so comfortable
in the *Marble Lounge*
for breakfast.

I want to stay here
and have them bring the
rest of Tokyo to me.

VII
Out of necessity
we learn that Buddhists
do, in fact, pee.

At Meiji Shrine

I
Long path from train
through gates, large like trees
A sea of umbrellas come

to visit the enshrined souls of
Emperor Meiji and his consort
the empress.

We wash hands
ritually like before a Jewish meal.
We bow and clap.

We drop coins in box.
People hang votive wood notes
like prayers in a Western Wall.

This is not an ancient place
But it is quiet like history.
Until young boy with his

bird sounds video game
forces us to move to a
more quiet corner.

The soul of the emperor
is broken up by rain drops.
We take him away in our wet clothes.

II
Young girl with Totoro Umbrella
visits Meiji Shrine. Totoro is
patron saint of umbrellas
and giant bunny as far
as I'm concerned.

III
I interrupt Addie's moment to say
I would like to have a beverage with owls now.
Without a word she waves her hand
summoning me to hand her the backpack.
Who who.

IV
There are many places
I'm not allowed entry to.
I'm thinking of converting so
I can get some better pictures.

At The Owl Village

They offer whiskey but
all agree it is best for me to

not have whiskey before
interacting with owls.

The owl village dog
steals the socks of the

patrons sitting on the
tatami mat.

I hold out newt for owls to eat.
They eat the meat.

They seem nervous.
They go for a walk every day

but otherwise
live in this room.

Legs connected
with owl leash to wood bars.

They sleep at night since
they don't have to hunt.

We vote for our favorite owl
which makes it feel like a

populowlity contest.
We both pick *Ohagi*.

The owls take a break
when we're done.

The dog makes noises
they prefer not to hear.

Cats Too

To be fair and true
to my nature, we pay 500 yen
to pet cats for ten minutes.

All the cats here look like
little emperors. They're used to
the hands of foreigners.

They're nonchalant about
the whole thing. Or that's
all cats, really.

We weren't excited that the time
it takes to put our possessions in the
lockers and put on and take off

the cat cafe slippers, counted
against our ten minutes.
But cats.

Bump of Chicken

At first I thought some restaurants
were getting a little too specific when
I saw one called *Bump of Chicken*
until I went to their website and saw that
it was a Japanese alternative rock group
at which point I thought that some band
names are getting a little too specific.

Wet

The rain has made it a hard day.
We crossed at Shibuya crossing
a few times and the look was
unique with all the umbrellas but
the wind and the rain made it
more cumbersome than enjoyable.
Then a toy store which Google
promised would be there, wasn't.
I can't let this get me down too much
as the robots are tonight and I
don't want them to sense my burden
and give me sad beeps and whirrs.
I'm as confident as all hell that
"beeps and whirrs" are the sounds
that robots make. I'm going to
dry off in the hotel and put on
the happiest American face I can
for the benefit of everyone visiting
the *Robot Restaurant* tonight.

Culture Shock

The Uber drivers wear suits here.
When I was a Lyft driver last summer
they were lucky if I wore pants.

At Robot Restaurant

It is important to note
robots neither dine
nor work here.

Robots are a state of mind.
One robot in the waiting area
who is not a robot

is a man dressed in robogalia
He plays Michael Jackson's
Man in the Mirror.

I guess *the news* hasn't
reached Japan yet.
Also the guitarist is

essentially a mirror.
They do not serve
domestic Whiskey here.

Robots only drink
whiskey from Tennessee.
Though a block or two east

They will serve you
the *Nikka* of your dreams.
I should get a drink

from any country to
get over this rain funk
and this *GPS doesn't work*

*near the tall
buildings of Tokyo*
funk.

These robots or
these robot people
better funk me up.

Oil can
Oil can
Oil can!

I'm a Poet Waxing Dark at a Robot Show

This is my burden.
A robot wants me to
drink popcorn.

What do you do?
I work at the Robot Restaurant
In Tokyo, is what some people
must say.

Lizards on the wall in one room.
Whatever they could find.

Protect your drinks from
big robots they warn us!

Three shows a day!
This was someone's
dream.

We see the contents of
the bento box next to us.
I want sushi not from
a robot restaurant Addie says
That's racist I tell her.

There will be two toilet breaks
during the show.

Please do not touch the robots

There's a whole lesson on leaning back so
the robots don't decapitate you.

A break is taken where souvenirs
are available. All I want from
the Robot Restaurant
is my hearing back.

Who wants a robot sundae?
Someone must.

Lucky Seat 113
gets a free giant popcorn
for no reason.

They cage us in for the second act.
It's getting very *Mad Max* in here.

The narrative is really coming
together now.

This is a whole different
level of ridiculous.

*Please turn off your WiFi devices
otherwise you're going to
mess up our robots.*

Act 3 – The narrative has
gone away again.

A family of *Darth Mauls* comes out
and they fight.
So that's kind of weird.

There's an uncomfortable amount
of Michael Jackson music

Finally, robots!

*The light sticks will not work
outside the restaurant!*

Fish fight! FISH FIGHT!

This show was an assault to all of my senses.
I want to have whiskey and see it again.

Please leave your seat now!!

We enter Shinjuku's *Mister Donut.*

My first question:
Is there a Mrs. Donut?

At Euphoria, Golden Gai

Nikka —
We are the only two people

but we fill the room where
bars are the size of

a single bar.
This is the smoothest

Japanese whiskey
I've ever had.

Tiya serves it to us.
We could open a bar

twice this size
in our guest room.

I notice Japanese
people have lips

or that could just be
the whiskey talking.

TOKYO DAY FOUR

武士

Good Morning, Shower

Water pressure
of dreams

Adjust to *my height*
Instant hot water

Make home shower
feel like caveman relic

Yesterday rinse away
Today's dreams

coated with
you

Handy at Breakfast

There's no easy way to eat these without getting lychee juice all over your hands Addie says referring to the bowl of lychees she has excavated from the breakfast buffet, in the wooden fruit bowl which they didn't have yesterday. Today I plan to get all over Addie's hands despite any local prohibition. There is no easy way not to.

At the Samurai Museum

I
I wonder if I can take
all the samurai swords
on the plane back
to America.

II
I tell the ticket sales person
I am only two years old
so I can get free admission.
He laughs at the absurdity of this
and says *doesn't look like.*

III
I *like* the museum on Instagram
to get a free sticker. I'll like anything
to get a free anything.

IV
I take a picture of
the sign that says
Let's take picture.

V
Our guide is called *Yu*
and he says we can call him
you.

VI
We learn *shogun* was
highest ranked
samurai.

VII
We learn teen samurai
would add fake mustache
made of horse hair
on their masks
to look older.

VIII
There is a lot of touching
happening around the many
no touching signs.

IX
*Samurai were typically short
so they would wear metal horns
to appear taller*

I typed while wondering
where I can get heightening horns
back in Los Angeles.

Maybe *Little* Tokyo.

X
Samurai would commit *hari-kari*
suicide cutting their stomach open
or beheading their co-samurai
when they realized they would lose
a battle rather than be captured
by enemy.

XI
We laugh at the sign that says
*please watch head over the
low doorway.*

XII
Addie notices the man with
the sushi socks and he says
dress for the occasion.

XIII
Samurai needs 3 skills in battle:
sword, archery, horse.

XIV
Three typhoons destroyed
three different Mongolian fleets
as they attempted to invade Japan.

XV
Kamikaze.
What they tried in Pearl Harbor.

XVI
Small armor on display
not for child samurai
but to display in house to
protect from bad health.

XVII
*Sign says
return used socks here*
Need signs back
in Van Nuys

XVIII
There was *horse sword*
and *ground sword.*

XIX
We learn ninja specialized
in assassination. They were like spies
while samurai were like soldiers.
Sometimes they would fight.
Sometimes work together.

XX
There were some women
in samurai period, I assume.
Otherwise no samurai babies.

XXI
Animal helmets
give samurai trait of animal –
Rabbit *fast.*
Lion *strong.*
Addie guesses *gremlin*
at one helmet.

XXII
They'd never seen a lion
So their depiction on helmets
was ideal as opposed to real.

XXIII
Samurai helmet
chin guard had
hole for summer sweat.

XXIV
Another *no touch* sign
but guide says *ok to touch*
so I put on head and he says
please do not wear.
Your guess is as good
as mine.

XXV
The sign with a hand
with red circle and bar
I think means *no touching*
but it could easily be
no waving.

XXVI
Addie is given task
of holding swords.
Japanese *samurai*
and Japanese *cute*
cultures collide.

XXVII
Guns were for killing horses
which makes me hate them
all the more.

XXVIII
Emperor Meiji retook power in 1868
and made it illegal to be a samurai
and now it is not possible to see
a real samurai, we learn.

XXIX
Yu runs to get extra swords
for the photos but walks
when he has them.

XXX
Regarding kimonos –
Left side always goes on top
otherwise means death.

XXXI
They help us
try on kimono
and samurai outfit
so we can
culturally appropriate
with their blessing

Pet Super Wan

We enter the kitten store
in Shinjuku and I swear to
Buddha we never leave.

Godzilla in Tokyo

I
Our first Godzilla sighting
on top of the roof of
the Toho Cinemas –
They just fed her so
we should be okay.

II
Godzilla roars
every hour
on the hour.

III
I'm standing at the intersection
of Godzilla Road and Western Civilization.
Actually this isn't an intersection
but a place where all things exist.
Godzilla IS western civilization
I hear her roar from the tops
of the buildings.

On the Marunouchi Line

A fat Japanese baby
eyes Addie suspiciously.
He has no idea what
he's missing.

At Honey Honey Cafe

I
I'm not allowed to touch the maids
at the maid cafe Addie tells me
citing their rules
and hers.

II
As best as I can tell
using Google Translate
Addie orders an omelet
with no blood pressure.

III
My prayer

Peace
No guns
Free health
Fix the elevator button
Everyone in kimonos
Rice with every omelet
Domestic whiskey
Cute socks
Kittens
Kittens
More kittens

IV
They draw kitten on top of my latte
in caramel and panda on top of
Addie's omelet in catsup.
This is why we came here.

V
Only men eating
and drinking here,
and Addie.

VI
Our first bidet-less toilet.
This is how cavemen
used to pee.

When on the train

*be conscious
of whether your
sound leaks*

Nakamise Shopping Street

I
Addie picks up a kitty towel and says
is this the hand towel I've been looking for.
I pick up a bag of chocolate pandas and
ask if this is the bag of chocolate pandas
she's been looking for.

II
Addie wants a massage
like the one she's seeing
in the pedestrian street.
But maybe not in the street
she clarifies.

III
Ladies in Kimonos Eating gelato.

Addie said it.
I just wrote
it down.

I Could Rewrite This as a Haiku But I'm Not Going To

Outside of the Sensō-ji temple
I drop off the last of the Mohicans
and finally enter Buddhist air space.

Source of Appropriation

The Nazi symbol
is everywhere – Reminds me
it was never *theirs*.

The Five Stories Pagoda

is indeed five stories.
Each one has its
own narrator.

This is Edo where the old
becomes older, where
the sound of wooden clogs

becomes holy, where the Buddha
takes his vacations.
To say there is something zen

about this place is
to say there is air in the air.
We breathe all of this.

Shadows

I'm sitting in the shadow
Of the Sensō-ji temple
which is sitting in
the shadow of the
Five Storied Pagoda
which itself is sitting
on the shadow of
the Tokyo Skytree
which sits in the shadow
of the sky.

A Couple of Google Translate Mishaps On Top of the Sky

I
He wanted to know if gelatin was okay
but Google asked us if *Johnny's Gelatin*
was okay. We wanted neither Johnny
nor gelatin in our food.

II
The best was when I asked if they normally served the bread
with olive oil, as opposed to butter which I thought would be
more typical for a French restaurant, and that they might have
misunderstood my dietary needs. I'm not sure what the waiter
wanted it to say, but Google told me it was *I am a virgin*.
Perhaps he just wanted to level with us. Don't worry Skytree waiter.
You'll find someone. And this olive oil was really good.

Finding My Limits

From the Skytree, the largest structure in Tokyo
and the largest broadcasting tower in the world,
you can not see the edges of Tokyo.

So much is person-made.
This city is the multiplication of New York
times Los Angeles.

It must have taken so may bricks
and so many pieces of metal.
How did they get all the pipes and wires?

I doubt I could make a single building.
Let alone all of this.
This is the final line of this poem.

Shortcut

I would like to zipline
from the top of the Skytree
back to Shinjuku
but the infrastructure for this
does not exist.

If We Could Fly

I tell Addie if we could fly
we'd save so much money
on metro tickets.

I have to clarify that
I am referring to the power of flight
and not becoming pilots.

Though I wonder
if you could fly yourself
if you would still be considered a pilot

even though you
weren't operating a plane.
Would the FAA require you

to get a license to operate yourself
or would they give you a pass because
they though it was cool?

Imposter Reflection

The reflection of things
on our hotel room table
appears on the ceiling –
Coins. iPhone Charging Case.
Wallet. Passport. Gift Bag.
Lamp head. Brochure.
I don't understand the physics of this.
There is no *under light* forcing its way
around the solid objects.
I don't understand the physics
of how I spend most of my days
seated in a chair with my fingers
on a keyboard, but have all the
energy needed to take every train
in Tokyo to every location in Tokyo.
The words *should we have breakfast
at seven a.m.* come out of my mouth
like an imposter. The Tokyo-Van Nuys Express
is re-writing my D.N.A.
We'll see who shows up at the airport
later this month.

A DAY IN HAKONE

箱根

This Morning

The shower water pressure
reminds me we should move
to this hotel to experience it daily.

The breakfast buffet too. Where
Addie's love affair with lychee fruit
continues. It's okay. Our marriage
has room enough for fruit.

And water pressure.

Walk to Train

I
I want to touch everything
next to *don't touch* signs.

II
We spot a sign in front of a
building in progress with a panda
dressed as a construction worker.
Addie squeals with excitement
and exclaims *I want a panda to
handle all my construction needs!*
Next on the agenda: find out what
Addie's construction needs are.

III
The Olympics are coming here in 2020
which has me wondering where they are now.
How do they dress when the world is
not watching. Will they wake up in time
to get here.

IV
Addie does a great impression
of what she would imagine someone
giving us the evil eye would be
after I worry someone may have just
spotted me touching her hand in public.
Imagine the cutest frog you've ever seen.
Yes, that's it.

On the Train to Hakone

I
We are seated in front of the *Romancecar
Limited Express* train to Hakone.
We don't like to put limits on our
romance but this train is a half hour
faster than the regular one. There
is volcanic activity in our immediate future
on the back of fifteen years of explosions
and lava flow.

II
I am eyes out the window for Mt. Fuji
but these clouds are telling me
the mountain does not want to
be seen today. She's so cute
when she pretends to be shy.

III
They say eating one of the black boiled eggs
extends your life by seven years.
I'm going to eat sixty of them and see
how this climate change thing pans out.

IV
Every Japanese
person head down in phone while
express train pass by.

V
Mr. Fuji boarded an
express train from Tokyo
and disembarked at Kawasaki.
Let the good times roll.

VI
Some restaurants say they are
vegetarian friendly. It doesn't mean they
have vegetarian food. It just means
they will be pleasant when they say
they have nothing for you to eat.

VII
Hakone Matata
is not a thing I should plan
on saying to everyone
I meet today.

VIII
I call every mountain I see from the train
Fuji. They are all too polite to correct me.

On the Train to Gora

I
This train is bound for Gora this train
This train is bound for Gora this train
This train is bound for Gora
Don't ride none but the dancing hora
This train is bound for Gora this train

II
Buddhist monks get in the train
not singing *hey hey were the monks...*
Addie says *give me that brain*
after I sing that out loud.

III
Scallops don't have brains
so you can't really have a good
conversation with them.

IV
This train
bound for Gora
is about to perform *switchbacks*.
It's not an open mic though so
passengers are requested
to not join in.

V
We're traveling through tunnels
built over a hundred years ago
that have withstood several
natural disasters. Back when
they really knew how to
build tunnels.

VI
Two trains in and no one
has checked our tickets
since we bought them.
We could be anyone from
anywhere riding to anywhere —
Transportation thieves
switching back like
Samurai and Clyde
Like Ninja and Capone
Like DB Hydrangea Cooper.
We're not though.

VII
The front conductor
switches places with
the back conductor
before every switchback.
This is either for safety
or they're punking us
with Japanese fire drills.

VIII
Mt. Fuji is three volcanoes
on top of each other, engaged in
a volcano orgy that has been
going on for millennia.

Picasso At the Hakone Open Air Museum

I
Plates

Face of Bearded Man
He's got an Eiffel Tower nose

Face, 1963
He's got a shrimp landed on his face nose.

Face, 1963
He's got a Roger Hargreaves nose
(Addie says *elephant*)

Face 1961
M and Z
He's got a Miyazaki nose.

Pot with Two Faces, 1952
Looking in opposite directions.
All lines of sight covered.

II
Etchings

*When I was the same age as those children,
I was able to sketch like Raphael. However, it took me
a lifetime to learn how to sketch like those children.*
　　　　　～ Pablo Picasso

At the Circus, 1905
Two naked people
Dance on a horse.

Two Heads of Women, 1908
I wonder if they're the naked dancers from
The previous etching.

Three Women, 1922-23
They've made a friend.

The Three Graces, 1922-23
They've taken off their
clothes again.

Two Nude Women, 1930
It didn't work out with the third woman.

Head of a Third Woman, 1938
You don't want to get on the bad side
of the other two women.

Monkey and a Reclining Nude, 1954
Addie has trouble identifying the monkey.

Woman with Her Hair in a Bun, 1957
Reminds me we need to try
those Japanese buns.

Musician, Man and Woman, 1967
The musicians trumpet is on display.

Reclining Amuse and Profiles, 1970
Most of the profiles are looking
at the reclining nude.

Seated Woman, 1972
She had all her defenses on display.

Nude Woman and Musketeer, 1972
It's a living.

At the Hakone Open Air Museum

I
We enter a sky hole
Addie's says *go into the sky hole
honey.* We could totally put a sky hole
in our yard in Van Nuys.

II
A little kid runs across a bridge
away from the Picasso building
yelling *charge!!!* I yell after him
Cash only!

Back at the Station

I
I'm pretty sure
1995 Yoko Ono
just got off the train.

II
When he was growing up
he may not have dreamed of
operating the cable car, but
he was born to do it.

Around Lake Asahi

I
I mix up the words *egg* and *boat*
which lead to a situation in which
we see ourselves floating on
Lake Asahi in a black smoked egg.

II
I tell Addie as we walk hand in hand
towards Hakone Shrine
that's how World War II started –
Two Americans showing public
displays of affection in the heart
of ancient Japan.

III
Leave it to the people in the goose pedal boat
to ruin the picture of the peace shrine gate
as they float on by in the background of
our zen photographic moment.

(Or they made it the perfect photo.)

IV
There's an Antoine de Saint Exupéry
museum in Hakone. I'd love to see it
as a fan of *Le Petit Prince*. Remind me
to look up his connection to Hakone
or Japan so I can stop wondering why
it's here.

Today

Today I took an express train
that went a long distance
A local train that switched
back and forth up a mountain
A cable car that did the job of five funiculars.
A bus that pretended to be a rope car
A pirate ship with no pirates
A long walk on my feet
on stones and between trees
A local bus that meandered
down the mountain
A reverse express train
My feet again
My piece of paper
that made it all possible

Faith

If I take a picture of a mountain
and tell you it is Mount Fuji
would you believe me?

Curry

It's Japanese curry night
in the Lupert household
two thirds of which has
travelled by dragon
to Shinjuku Station
where more people go
where they are going
than any other place
where people go.

Tired Words

Addie has gotten to the point
in her level of tiredness where
she's replacing all her consonants
with "n"s. She tells me she's *nired*
and I tell her *I'm norry to near nhat*.
It gets really good when she adds
an "s" to that and tells me to *snop it*.

Mr. Nobuaki Takahashi

Mr. Nobuaki Takahashi
of Comorebi –Saudade-
in Golden Gai closed out
our day over premium
Japanese whiskey.
He has a guitar on
the wall and a daughter
eleven months old
at home. *Both expensive*
he tells us. He serves
the finest whiskey in Japan
but his drink is Yellow Rose
of Texas Bourbon. He says
Maker's Mark (a commoners
brand in the U.S. [and my favorite])
is expensive. This is his
daily bourbon, though he only
serves scotch and
Japanese whiskey
in his store. He knows
what he is talking about
and he will tell it to you
if you want. The olympics
are coming and he hopes
business will pick up.
He makes music.
His daughter, still
eleven months old,
bangs on a piano
in a video for us.
Mr. Nobuaki Takahashi
is the Golden Gai.
You should give him
all your money
in exchange for
the water
of life.

TOKYO LAST DAY
江戸

Standard

We're leaving
one of the great breakfasts
of our time today.

Leaving for
breakfasts unknown. Breakfasts
we'll be comparing to this one,

breakfast of emperors.
breakfast you'll write
poems about.

This coffee.
These lychee.
This French toast.

These little, tiny, small, minuscule
Japanese mushrooms. So very
not big.

Except for the
space they take up
in our hearts.

After Three Cups

Coffee is liquid so
I'm feeling pretty
hydrated today.

Subway

I
As much as I appreciate
the expansiveness of Tokyo's
transportation options
I'd much rather be traveling by
Miyazaki's Cat Bus.

II
The Marunouchi subway line is
now rolling above ground which
defies all my beliefs about what
subways should be doing.

It's possible I wrote a
similar poem with a similar
sentiment, in a similar city which
appears in a similar book.

III
I did. It is in the book
Nothing in New England Is New
on Page 107

Serenity

Addie wonders what the writing
on my T-shirt is. It is easy to think
that it is Japanese as we are in Japan

but I think it is Mandarin.
It is from the program *Firefly* where,
in space, they sometimes spoke Mandarin.

We are on a crowded train
and can't hold up the translation box
to inspect my shirt in these conditions.

If all goes well there will be a note
below this on the page revealing
the secrets of my space shirt

which will be revealed
at a later time.

All did not go well.

Train People

I
Their lips are so red
these Japanese women.
Their hair so black.
They wear tatami mat
sandals on their feet
while they use their red
iPhones to communicate
with the future.

II
Addie wants to know
all the secrets
of the boy
with the 420 tattoo
on his arm
and the bag with
the lion mouth face.

At Edo-Tokyo Museum

I
Words the docent said
in some context or other:
Gorgeous
Less gorgeous
Simple

II
The great fire of 1657
lasted for three days
destroyed sixty percent of the city
killed a hundred thousand people

III
The 16th Shogun
was the first photographed.
He was not allowed
to be called *Shogun*
as the title was abolished.
His descendants
still exist.

IV
I guess correctly when
our guide, *Yushika,*
asks how long it takes
to walk from Tokyo (Edo)
to Kyoto – *Two weeks.*
She is excited by my accuracy
and there is a round of high fives

V
Shintoism Japan indigenous
Shrines Shinto

Temples Buddhist
Shrines Towers

Temples Pagodas
Yushika says

Shrines celebrations
Temples funerals

VI
The palanquin, which looks like
the Ark of the Covenant, was used to
carry men and women around.
The one for women was
much more ornately decorated.
This is how Addie will
travel from now on.

VII
Old Edo rooms were measured
by the number tatami mats you
could fit on their floors.

VIII
Commoners slept
in the same rooms
they ate, worked
and taught in.

IX
Everyone laughs after I tell them
I just need a minute
in front of the Edo-era toilets
just as I had planned.

X
We see a display of famous banned books
The alarm goes off when I walk by.

XI
The moveable soba stand
I want to move home with me.

XII
Addie demands I carry her when
she gets in the palanquin, but I get
out of the responsibility when we realize
this is the one for men.

XIII
A Quick Summary of All Japanese History

There was craziness for a long time
Then the shogun with their samurai took over.
Then the emperor got the power back
and along came the subways and everyone
shook hands with the west.

XIV
The commoners visit the stories
of their ancestors. We are only
allowed in because Emperor Meiji
said it should be so.

XV
This is how we'll travel tonight
I say in my fancy voice when we
encounter one of the Kanda Myōjin
Shrine floats.

XVI
The new Meiji government
wanted to imitate London and Paris
and be a city that does not burn.
Brick walls went up everywhere.

XVII
Panda Coin Bank made of Soft Vinyl, 1970

If it were up to Addie we'd put
all our money into pandas.

XVIII
We walk the wrong way into
the *Modern Tokyo* exhibit and watch
automobiles and iMacs devolve into
burnt cities and Shogun warriors.

XIX
I tell Addie we went the wrong way
and are seeing history in reverse.
That's okay she says, I know how it ends
which may be the most ominous
thing that's ever come out of her mouth.

XX
They skip right over the whole
*and then we decided to bomb
Pearl Harbor* piece and get right
into air raids over Tokyo.

Pants are the Future

I'm reminded of earlier today when
the man at the baggage storage
facility in Tokyo Station told me to
pick up our luggage before 8pm
or else I'd be wearing *inside out pants*.
That was his suggestion to me
after I thought I'd be wearing no pants
if we didn't come in time.

Geometry PSA

Addie wants everyone to know that the things they call rice balls in the Lawson Markets are actually rice triangles.

Dust in Space

I read a poem by Dorianne Laux
while on a train to Tokyo Disneyland
Resort, or rather our hotel there so
we can sleep enough to spend
a day paying our obligatory tributes.
The poem is about how the world
came from dust and eventually
will just be a rock again,
floating in space with no
memories of anything we did
like picking oranges or breathing.
So, I'm not making any long term
plans and just want to know if
I should go on the Winnie the Pooh ride
first like one person recommended
even though that doesn't make
sense to me. Maybe I'd better do it
before Winnie and all his friends
are dust again – dust in space with
no one left to sweep it up.

At the Hotel

They make me put on gym shorts *for your safety* in the fitness room at the Hilton Tokyo Bay. I want to launch into a dissertation on my history at Hilton fitness rooms and emphatically explain how I've never been required to wear shorts for my rigorous five minutes of lifting weights. But I remember this is how World War II started and she's willing to give me the rental shorts for free because I'm a *Gold* member and it's so close to closing time. So I relent and wrap her gift shorts around my legs so I can do what I need to do and make my father, the fitness king of South Florida, proud.

Night Cap

I
In the Silver Lounge at the hotel
I order a Japanese Whiskey I haven't
tried yet...Yamizake (no relation)
and they serve it to me in a glass
almost as big as my head, which
if you know me, is already pretty big.
I wish I could tell you they made up
for the gargantuaness with
a pour generous enough to warrant
a glass this size, but alas (a word
they use in telling stories like the ones
we'll immerse ourself in tomorrow)
it is not so. I shouldn't complain as
you can't judge a whiskey by
it's vessel, and there are waterfalls
surrounding me, and a plate of
cashews taking care of all my
other needs. Addie is upstairs
sewing a hole in the backpack
which Amazon gave us for free.
Our son, who loves any mention
of nuts, especially if the word *hot*
precedes it, is across an ocean.
I can't imagine what he's doing
right now. Actually, yes I can.
I'm pretty good at imagining things.

II
For Jude
I'm not sure these nuts are the
right taste bud companions for
this whiskey. Haha. I said *nuts.*

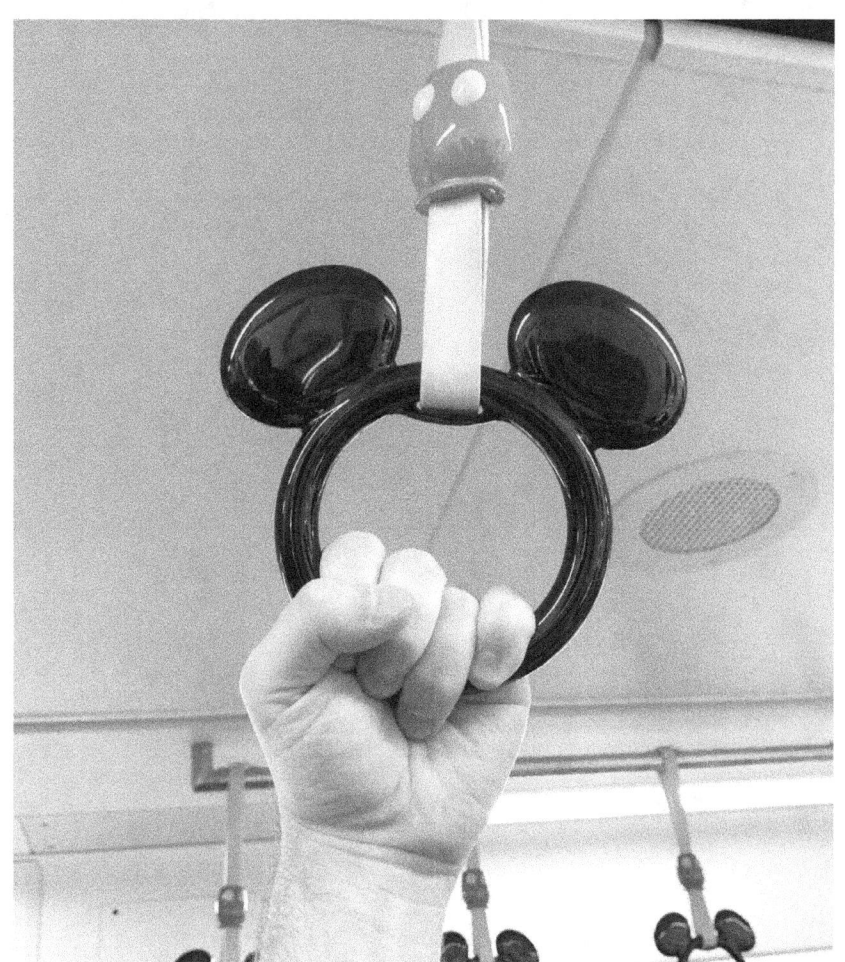

A DAY AT TOKYO DISNEYLAND

鼠

Amazing

I can see Space Mountain
outside our hotel window.

They really know how to do
water pressure in these

Japanese hotels. The large
mirror has a space that heats up

so when you're done there's a square
that hasn't been steamed over.

Addie foreshadowed this
with "the most amazing thing

you're going to experience is
right here" pointing to the mirror

before I showered. All I could see
was myself. I took it as an affirmation

This is the most amazing thing.

At Breakfast

Chim chiminey…and other
Disney classics in Japanese
shower over us as we drink
the coffee which isn't as
good as the other place, and
dine on plates, by our choice,
from the kids station with
character compartments
that remind us of home.
The Tokyo-Van Nuys Express
is boarding the monorail
for tomorrow.

At Tokyo Disneyland

I
Japanese Tigger —
We're about to get
in a honey pot

II
*Please do not accept
packages from any
unknown life form.*

III
Much of the initial narration
of *Pirates of the Caribbean*
is in Japanese, until they get to
Dead men tell no tales
at which point it changes to
original pirate *arrnglish*.

IV
Popcorn in
anything you can
imagine.

V
On *Space Mountain*
they have balls I can touch.
They're not as big as
the ones in Anaheim.

VI
I tell Addie she has to see these Tigger shirts
in case she hasn't already. She's much more
likely to spot Tigger shirts before me.

VII
The graves are fresh
at the Haunted Mansion.
The one of Fluffy the Cat
has nine different dates of death.

VIII

I want to experience the
Deadwood narration version of
Big Thunder Mountain.

IX

Addie is on the lookout for
alien mochi dumplings.
I'm not sure if that's
something they have here, or
if she's having an episode.

X

The menu at *Blue Bayou*
under the vegetarian choice says
You can also eat vegetarians.
I feel we should avoid this place.
(Though I am compelled to ask
if the vegetarians are vegetarian.)

XI

Country Bear Jamboree –
A bear fell in love with an octopus
Was that in the original script?

XII

Lots of people are
groups of people dressed
exactly like each other
walking down the Disney
streets, holding hands.

XIII

A parade has characters
we don't recognize. A red devil
leading a float. *That's Japanese
Satan* are the words that come
out of my mouth that cause
Addie to shake her head.

XIV

I saw Peter Pan on one of the
parade floats while we were in
line for his ride. I hope he gets
back here in time for us to see
him in Neverland.

XV
Addie fixes my umbrella
which had broken into
four pieces somewhere
near the Jungle Cruise.

XVI
Get ready for the Jungle Cruise
in Japanese! (The back side of water
is a universal concept.)

XVII
Addie is wrapped up in
the world of the sleeping baby
resting her head on her
mother's shoulder.

XVIII
The Jungle Cruise
goes the other way
which I am not
prepared for.

XIX
My options here are to
laugh whenever the
Japanese people laugh
or to offer to translate
my memories of the
Jungle Cruise script
into English.

XX
We close it out with *Small World*.
It's a good one. We've been to
four Disneylands on three continents
and we always end with *Small World*.
It's a good one…after all.

You

You with your fists around the wine glass stems
You walking by with your luggage
You with the bundles in your hair
You bringing the pizza
You who had to go to another floor
      for the asparagus
You who revel in the waterfall
You with the orange jacket
You who works here
You from another country
You whose crust is soft like a pillow
You who demands more than silence
      from the elevator
You who crushed the grapes
You whose head as big as glass
You who fall asleep
You who sleep
You

A DAY SPENT TRAVELING TO KYOTO

新幹線

The Japanese

must think us all cavemen
us Americans with our
rampant bidet-less toilets.

It's raining again

like it did yesterday
and several days ago.
We're heading to the west
or, by our eyes, the south –
Kyoto by a train they
named after what
comes out of a gun.
I'm dressed in silver today
so I can blend in.
Breakfast closes at ten.
We've got one more minute
in this part of civilization.

The coffee is good today.

Unlike every other time in
this hotel (which was only
yesterday) when it was
just okay. We have a short
but detailed history, this hotel,
this coffee, and us.

Concierge

I ask for a bandaid and I'm not sure if she understands so I do a demonstration and I think she now wants to help me cut off my finger.

While Waiting for the Bus to the Train

I
We miss the bus to the train station.
But another one will come. Tokyo
is all about moving people from
one place to the other in one
vehicle or another. Another one
will always come.

II
Everyone smokes in Tokyo.
Actually very few people
smoke in Tokyo. It's
definitely one of the two.
Or somewhere in between.

III
I don't think our Kyoto hotel
has a fitness room so I may
have to lift Addie in the air
a hundred and five times
to maintain all of this.

IV
I'm just here with my brain
waiting for a bus. It's all
starting to come out.

V
In case you're trapped behind
a wall of 50 Yen coins, don't
worry – You can just look through
the holes to see if rescue is coming.

On the Train to the Next Train

I
The adult boy on the train
with the magnificent Japanese hair
gives a long sigh with his head
buried in his phone. It could be
a specific piece of information
he's seeing or just the tremendous
weight of everything that's
led him to this moment
on this train.

II
Later he picks his nose and
I'm no longer interested.

III
The rings for holding onto
hanging from the train
ceiling bars aren't the same
when they're not shaped
like Mickey's hands.

"eating"

a found poem

Eating that is important for people to live on.
At Mumokuteki Cafe, I would like to cook the

taste of nature as it is and to deliver a small
impression and relief to everyone's life.

We want to share the peace of mind of
our crops and we want to deliver richness

to our loved ones.
There are places where vegetables and

rice are born as well as us, and there are
producers who face the area and nature

that they have grown.
I think that what is good for the body and

the environment that Mumokuteki Cafe aims
is an important role to convey to the future

the smell of the earth, the creator's feelings,
and the connections of people through one food.

Thoughts While Riding a Bullet

I
Every Bridge
in Japan is a
Japanese bridge.

II
The English translation on
one restaurant's website menu
in addition to *vegetarian friendly*
says *kids available*. I'll have
two little girls, and throw in
a little boy for the amuse bouche.

III
The sun has
been in Kyoto
this whole time.

IV
Does the bullet train go
as fast as a bullet or does
a bullet go faster?

V
Do they look from the houses
to the train as longingly as I
look at the houses from the train?

VI
Kyoto
Ancient capital
Tokyo-Van Nuys Express
rolling in to you.

On Another Train

Another dad tells his son
maybe eight years old, that
It will take three hours with no breaks
for water or bathrooms to walk
from the train to the hotel.
He's lying, of course, and his son
knows it. I tell him we're on the
same dad plane of existence
in terms of how we lie to our
sons for the sake of being
hilarious and to take in the
looks of suspicious disbelief
on their faces. This is the fuel
we live on, us dads.

Fortune

I'm going to make my fortune in Japan, suing everyone who uses the word Rick-shaw.

In Oagari Restaurant, Kyoto

I
One of our dishes is served with
what looks like a branch of miniature
Japanese maple leaves. We wonder
if we can eat these and I encourage
Addie to give one a try. She says
it tastes like tree. This news that
Addie knows what trees tastes like
opens up a mystery about her past.
How do you know I ask her.
I know she responds
definitively.

II
Because of a fancy font
I misread the IWAI Whiskey bottle
as *TWAT Whiskey*
How do they make that
I wonder.

III
We discuss how things
are translated with one of
the twenty-eight year old
owners of Oagari where
they served us food
that we want to eat
again and again.

We tell him the story of
how the waiter in
Tokyo told us
I am a virgin

We tell him his
restaurant menu should
probably say *kids menu available*
instead of just *kids available.*
He doesn't want to change
the website menu as he
thinks it's funny like I do.

He tells us where to get ramen
and what part of town to go to
to dine on top of the river.

I tell him my name is *Rick*
because he met his co-owner
when they were both rickshaw
drivers. He is old and new combined.

He has just returned from Phuket
where he hurt his foot on the beach
like me who just hurt my foot on
the raised platform of the tatami
mat floor in our room.

He said the food in Thailand is more
concerned with taste than presentation,
unlike in Japan where it is more about
presentation. He wants both for Oagari
and we confirm that is what we received.
Both.

We're in a different world now
where kids come with the meal
(if you believe the menu)
where the food is food
we'll remember as long
as we can open our mouths.

Maiko Prep

Before the Maiko show I tell Addie
she can get a Maik-over if she wants to.
Although what I'm saying is factual
she gives me that look of *I heard what*
you just said and this 'look' is the
only acknowledgement that's coming.

The Maiko Show in Our Hotel

I think is happening in the breakfast room
Or maybe breakfast happens in the maiko room.

Our maiko, or geisha in training
or *gaiko* in training in Kyoto dialect

is four years into it.
She paints herself white, even

the straight thin necked lines
on the back. She tells us

this July hair is all *her* hair.
Her upper and lower lips are rouged

unlike a first year maiko who
may only rouge her bottom lip.

Our maiko's collar is white
indicating she is closer to gaiko

then younger maikos whose colors
are many colors.

Maikos are more cute.
Gaikos are more elegant.

The white makeup started when
there wasn't lighting as a method for

the audience to see the performers
at night. We see our maiko at night.

She says she has no plans to stop.
She may be a gaiko all her life.

KYOTO DAY ONE

武士

Happy Pancake

I
I think we humiliate ourselves at
Happy Pancake describing our
understanding of the difference
between *big* and *small* in terms
of cups of coffee. Our waitress
reports something to two other
staff and they laugh until the
end of the Edo period.

II
No one is happier
than our waitress
at Happy Pancake.

III
No one is happier than Addie,
who hasn't had pancakes in
a gluten free minute,
at Happy Pancake.

IV
I keep banging my phone into things
and dropping it. We're at the point where
Addie wants me to throw it in the river
and get it over with.

V
Addie is off to watch them
make the pancakes. She hears
they deflate so you should take
the picture quickly.

VI
Addie, with her newly positioned hair bundles,
wants to know if she looks cute, or like a bug.
Why can't it be both, honey bee?
Why can't it be both?

VII
It takes twenty minutes
to make the pancakes.
They don't tell you it
also takes twenty minutes
to bring you coffee. They
laugh when they bring it
which either makes up for it
or deepens the humiliation.

VIII
The American mother
behind us is so off on her days.
She isn't convinced today
is Sunday. Oh it's Sunday lady
the day your family's loud forks
create a world war against your plates.
Where in the empire is my
goddammed coffee?!

IX
I want my coffee
so bad I want my coffee
so bad I want my

X
Now every time a noise happens
the immediate response is
throw it in the river!

Notes from the Kyoto Free Walking Tour

I
A dozen Ferrari's drive by
before the tour starts.

II
Today's kabuki involves
no *side business* like
the two previous banned versions.

III
Real geisha are
not the ones walking
down the streets
with photographers.

IV
Our guide speaks
five languages fluently.
I barely speak English
fluently.

V
We're not the only ones
says Addie spotting a
kipah on another tour
participant's head.
My entire book is
coming out of her mouth.

VI
It costs 750,000 Yen
to have an evening in
the most expensive tea house
with a geisha, in Gion.

VII
*What is said in the tea house
stays in the tea house.*

VIII
Tea house is just a name
like at the coffee houses in Amsterdam
where you don't go to get coffee.

IX
*Japanese don't have
so much touching culture.*
So don't rush to embrace
a geisha or maiko.

X
There are no garbage bins
in Japan to avoid people
putting explosives in them.

XI
Tanuki –
My little friend
is a raccoon.
He has big eyes for luck
and a big belly.

XII
They start to train at fifteen or sixteen
after middle school. High school
is not obligatory.

XIII
Eighty thousand geisha
before the war. Now
about two thousand.

XIV
The rules are important to
all Japanese. They wouldn't
dream of crossing even
the smallest, car-less street
until the light turned green.

XV
It is rude to walk in the street
eating food. Except during festivals.

XVI
She can't emphasize enough –
No side business.

XVII
Shintoism has no central deity.
They worship everything natural.

XVIII
The Japanese mix and match
Shintoism and Buddhism
and, now, other religions.
For example, for Christmas
they all go to a Kentucky Fried Chicken
because Colonel Sanders
looks like a Santa Claus.

XIX
Buddhists walking down the street
in their Buddhist outfits cross paths
with tourists walking up the street
in our tourist outfits.

XX
The path to the
oldest part of Kyoto
passes through some of
the newest buildings.

XXI
Yasaka Kōshindō Temple
is very monkey heavy.
Attention Judaism:
I'd like more monkeys
involved with ritual.

XXII
Each floor of the pagoda
represents a different event
of nature. It is possible some
of Buddha's ashes are here.

XXIII
We pass a rickshaw driver.
I want to ask him if he's going
to open a restaurant and if
I get to ride for free.

XXIV
We explain to the guide why
we're in Japan. The whole story
of how we had a child ten years ago
when we first thought we'd come
but then we got pregnant. (I clarify
that mainly Addie was pregnant.)
Now he's at camp for three weeks.
She says *two weeks is a good amount of time
to get an overview of the country.*
We're standing in front of
Higashiyami bathrooms and I
interrupt our conversation to say
I have to pee. Perfect she says in
her perfect Barcelonian accent.

XXV
There are temples everywhere here.
But few, if any, with Torahs.
There are shrines everywhere here.
You can worship anything you want.

XXVI
We visit the most important tree
in Maruyama Park. It blossoms
when it is time to blossom.
It feels pretty good about
its importance. Now is not
the time when it blossoms.

We May Miss out on the Sake Museum

That's okay.
I'm going to build
one at home.

Soon Enough References to World War II in This Book Will Not Be Intended With Humor

Addie wonders if she can wear
sneakers with a kimono so she
can have the experience but
still be comfortable walking.
Yet another opportunity to tell her
that's how World War II started.

Rain

It is hard work typing
everything I think with
one hand while the other
holds an umbrella.

Nishiki Market

Nishiki market sells
everything you can imagine
and a lot of things your
imagination has not
come up with yet
but that will haunt you
for the rest of your life.

Back in the Wild West

I message Brendan to tell him he's
going to need to get rid of all of his stuff
to make room for all the Japanese things.
Every object screams his name. I've already
shipped him Mt. Fuji.

He writes back wondering how I
feel about pine cones and deer scented
body lotion. I think he's in a forest
or is just trying new things in Hollywood.

Much of what we do is sit at tables
where there is food and hand each other
objects. We wrap the objects in papers
that the other carefully disassembles

so the other can use the same paper
later on. There are frequent choruses of
I remember that paper over coffee.
He still hasn't finished the Ireland

I sent him. I'm still getting through
a bag of jelly beans from New York City
that seems to refill itself. I'd bet he'd want
to know why all the stanzas in

this poem have four lines except
the first one which has five. That
extra line is a gift from Japan.
It's one of the many many things.

At the End of a Kyoto Day

We slurp the noodles at Engine Ramen
We put our umbrellas in the places where they go
We walk the covered walkways as much as possible
We glue our toes together with bandaids
We almost fall asleep typing words
We eat *Melonpan*
We dip in the hot bath
We do what people who
are like us do
Enough said
Enough said

KYOTO DAY TWO
着物

In the City of Kyoto

I'm eating breakfast in the
Japanese city of Kyoto.

I'm walking to the kimono store
in the streets of the city of Kyoto.

The elevators are speaking to me
in the city of Kyoto.

The raccoons here are known
for their large and magical testicles.

The raccoons in the city of Kyoto
which may not be raccoons at all.

Kimono

Addie is trying on a kimono which
we have purchased. It is a special
summer kimono known as a *yukata*
made of cotton and lighter than
the more traditional silk.
The person here held up two
kimono belts. One white and one
yellow. *Beautiful or cute* she asks.
We select white, beautiful, even though
Addie already has both of these covered.
If you're going to Kyoto City
be sure to wear a chopstick in your hair
or maybe a flower or both.
Either way you won't match the beauty
of what you're wrapping up.

Floors

There are two types of floors in Japan. The ones you are required to take your shoes off before walking upon, and the ones which you are not.
Of the latter, you can add a subcategory of all the ridges in the sidewalks that make you wish you could float to your destination.

5 7 3

I've given myself
a haircut in the city
of Kyoto.

At the tea ceremony

we are going to,
you can pay an extra fee
to wear a kimono.

I wonder if you
wear your own Kimono,
if there is a *bring*

your own fee, like a
cake cutting fee or corkage.

Time will reveal to
us the answer to this
question.

haiku

The prettiest girl
I know wears kimono on
bus ride to drink tea.

Generalization

Japanese people,
it seems, in particular
bus drivers, which

admittedly, is
only a small segment of
the Japanese population,

don't like to finish their
sentences. They hold out the
last syllable like

a long musical
note so the information
can flow into your

ears
like a
song.

Riding the Bus is easier

than I thought it would be.
Finding the bus stop was the
hardest part.

Buses can turn anywhere
and how do you identify where
to get off in a foreign country.

The trains go on tracks
(as if you didn't know that)
and don't take lefts or rights

like buses are free to do.
But this bus has screens in English
which tell you what stop is next,

so there's no guesswork
or concern about understanding
what the driver is saying.

I am filled with confidence
on this bus and the easiest part
is sitting in the seat,

the actual act of riding.
The left turn we just took
doesn't bother me at all.

P.S. Who am I to give the bus such
an easy pass? Yesterday we boarded
an express train and ended up in 1868.

They're Everywhere

If you don't want to travel far
to get to a temple or shrine
just go to the one which is
undoubtedly within twenty five feet
if you are in Kyoto.

Not Edible

Incense is packaged like boutique chocolate bars so be careful what enters your mouths no matter how intriguing it smells.

At the Tea Ceremony

I
When I ask if I should
wear the slippers on the mat
she says *we wear nothing.*
This tea ceremony just got
interesting.

II
Everyone is equal in the tea room
I will join you
Excuse me for going before you
Thank you for the tea

III
Actually we don't talk
during the tea ceremony
Ashe tells us after four
Americans tell each other
everything.

(This is how World War II started)

IV
The tea container is
shaped like a monster who comes
out of the river.

V
The tea room
is four and a half
tatami mats.

VI
Guests never whisk their own tea
but we are here for an experience
and that experience is provided.

Sake

Out of respect to all
the wineries and breweries
and distilleries we've set foot in
we're going to the Sake Museum.

Sake is a gentle liqueur.
It arrives sweet on your tongue
but it works in your blood

like all the other drinks
you know.

On the Way to the Sake Museum

I
We haven't had to wait long
for any transit. They just want
you to go where you are going
as fast as you can go.

II
Did we get into a Japanese garden
you ask? *The whole country is
a Japanese garden* I answer.

III
A large man on train
eyes my wife's rice ball. This is
not a metaphor.

IV
Addie wants to fly the little woman
who dressed her this morning home
for all future kimono dressing needs.
Even with our Van Nuys guest room
it seems like that may be too
much of a luxury for us.

V
Addie spots Waldo next to an owl.
You found him I shout!

At the Okura Sake Museum

I
They request you taste the sake
AFTER the tour.

II
The rice they use is from California.
We could have brought some for them
and maybe bartered our way in.

III
The process of preparing the wet rice
with bare feet reminds Addie of
that famous *I love Lucy* episode
with the grapes.

IV
They chant as they
stir the steamed rice.

V
Hatsu-zoe - day 1
Odori - day 2
Naka-zoe - day 3
Tome-zoe - day 4

VI
We see the biggest sake bottle.

VII
The *how to make sake* part
of the museum stops when they
get to the milky substance part
of the process. The mystery of
the clear liquid in the bottle
still eludes us.

VIII
Our phone translator tells us
one sake is *Breeding Sake*.
Now we know why there are
so many people in Japan!

Japanese Language Boat Trip to Nowhere

We take a boat which reminds us
of the Jungle Cruise only it's
fifty minutes instead of five.

They don't take cards for boat tickets
Only money.

The tour is only in Japanese.
Distorted Japanese because of the
dirty potentiometer.

This may not have been our
best decision but the boat
was leaving in two minutes so
it was do or die.

Remind me to look up the
name of this river.

It's called the Uji River
I looked it up.

The only thing our translating app
picked up was *it was full of people
of the north.*

This is how the Japanese do it.

the tour guide sounds like
he knows what he is talking about.
Especially when he talks over the
prerecorded narration.

The only things in English were
the sign telling us where the boat tour starts,
the woman who said *only money*
and the signs in the park they brought us to
which said *if you are on the boat
do not leave the park.*

I get scolded in Japanese
upon entering the return boat
when I accidentally lift up
a life jacket.

The job of the person in the
front of the boat is to stare
at the water and do nothing
while the person in the
back of the boat does
all the work.

No one looks at or talks to
Addie and me. This is how
World War II started.

Up and down the Uji River
these boats go all day
for no particular reason.

Well at least
we got to go
on a boat.

Testimonials

I'm not wearing the right shoes for rain, Addie says.

I'm not the right human being for rain, Rick says.

Dragon Burger

My train of thought
which I'm vocalizing out loud
about whether we're on the right train
is interrupted (seamlessly) by the words
Dragon Burger. It's Addie's turn to
think I might be having a seizure
but really I'm just reading the name
of a restaurant on a billboard
we're passing.

Tofubilities

We have dinner at a tofu restaurant
that an article said would do more things
with tofu than we ever thought possible.
I don't know how much time I've spent
imagining the possibilities of tofu
to accurately agree with this
but we did enjoy the meal
a lot.

Fall

I fell down a couple of stairs at the restaurant today.
I was fine but everyone who worked there came
running – several servers, the chef from the kitchen
an older woman, her daughter, her daughter's friends.
Socks on wooden stairs. There's always the possibility
a slippery step will have the entire empire running
in your direction.

Obi Dobi Do

Addie has been judging the amount of food
she's taken in today, by how tight the kimono belt
feels wrapped around her. I think she called it
an *obi*. The obi (pronounced ooh-bee) sits below the
booby (pronounced boo-bee). I think a letter is
removed as you get lower on the body
kind of like a reverse zipper song.
A zipper song is not a song about zippers
(though it could be) but rather a song where
one word or line of the song changes to
create a new verse, where the rest of the words
remain the same. Zipper songs are great
for sing-alongs because once you know
how it goes, you can easily change one
word or phrase without learning an entirely
new verse. If you'd like to know more about
zipper songs, try doing a search on the internet.
This is a book about Japan and I've run out of
space to continue this kind of tangent.

Help Me

The Tokyo-Van Nuys Express has
no idea where it's having breakfast tomorrow.
Or there are a couple of ideas but
half of the decision making team
has fallen asleep. That half of the team
also woke up a half hour into sleeping
to announce she was going to sleep.
Now that I've said *she* you probably
have a pretty good idea what is going on here.
Since you're so smart and deductive
maybe you can tell me where we're
having breakfast tomorrow.
I'm tired of making decisions.

KYOTO DAY THREE

漫画

Morning Scheme

Now's our chance I tell Addie
when I see the stacks of clean towels
in the fourth floor hallway of our hotel.
We could make our fortune selling towels!
To who? She wants to know, and it
takes me a minute to compose myself
before I reply *wet people*
with such pride at the simplicity
of my answer. I can't see her
reaction or even if there was one
as she's already in the elevator
pressing buttons to move on
from this madness.

Missing Canadians

Whatever happened to our
best friends the Canadians who
live in Australia who we shared
three trains with and encountered
three separate times on the
streets of Gion? The family
with the dad who shared a
wavelength with me – Who
has inspired me to tell Addie
it would take two hours to
walk there with no water or
breakfast, uphill, no matter
whenever she asked how long
it would take to get somewhere?

Whatever happened to our
best friends the Canadians with
no discernible Australian accent
which is how we found out they're
from Canada and not originally
from Australia as they'd been
telling us.

I'll tell you what happened.
A dragon swallowed them up.
A giant crab near the Nishiki market.
A Godzilla in Shinjuku.
We'll never see the Canadians again.
(These particular Canadians.)
I'll carry their torch as we wait
in this long morning line to
drink coffee they say is
smarter than us.

Before Coffee Query

*Do you think they kidnapped that crying baby
and are disguised as a family* I ask Addie
who is in desperate need of coffee before she can
deal with anything that comes out of my mouth.

At Coffee Smart

Addie keeps telling me things like
I hear the egg sandwiches need salt
and *I hear they bring a syrup to
put in the coffee.* I'm wondering
what secret conversations she's
been having about *Coffee Smart*
and with whom, and what else
is going on.

At the Manga Museum

I
Preschoolers get into the museum free.
Despite me making a solid case,
they do not let me in free.

II
A timeline tells us that it is around 49 years of age
that *Yakudoshi* (unlucky year) happens for men
when, it is considered that, catastrophe can *easy occur.*

III
I put headphones on to
listen to Japanese explanations.

IV
The first sign refused to define what manga is
but welcomed my definitions.
I may charge an admission fee to give my answer.

V
Manga and anime
in a way are married.

VI
Manga are fundamentally shaped by principles,
but on the whole, most readers are unconscious
of that fact.

VII
Gag Manga typically ends with a punchline.
Like much of my gag poetry.

VIII
One style of drawing is called *Manga without the Manga.*
There are a lot of empty panels involved.

IX
Who decided that the time in manga and reality are different?
Who decided that only the important actions should be drawn?
Who decided the reading order of the panels?
There are many *who decided* questions
posted in the museum continuing the
we don't know what the hell this is
theme of the place.

X
Are Manga artists millionaires?
Short answer: mostly no.

XI
The Rose of Versailles (Berusaiyu No Bara)
Riyoko Ikeda

Looks a lot like the captain fish guy from Miyazaki's *Ponyo*.

XII
Is cosplay manga?
Everything is manga.
Your breakfast toast is manga.
Your underwear is manga.
Your pencil and hair products are manga.
Everything is manga.

XIII
I reach a small display
of adult manga - fan made.
I respectfully barely look at it.
For a while.

XIV
The thickness of the books
is not unrelated to the reading speed
of the readers.

XV
Manga has taken over the world.
Manga is already in your town.
You probably had manga for breakfast.
Manga is in France.
Your eyes on these words is
a form of manga.

XVI
There are plaster models of
manga artist hands on display.
I'd like a plaster model of
my brain on display and
the sooner the better!

XVII
Some of the artists whose plaster
hands are on display also
contributed a drawing on
display next to their hands.
Some did not, leaving us
looking at just a hand, and
a pen, and a possibility.

XVIII
One picture
Beard man
No mouth
Just beard

XVIX
The *doughnut phenomenon*
is when city population hollows
out of city centers. In my world
the doughnut phenomenon is
when I see a doughnut and
need to eat it.

XX
Tatsuike Primary Schook's
A selection of "nostalgic textbooks"
is on display for those prone to
sentiment like me.

XXI
The poem of wind and trees
Virgin Rabbit
Takemiya Keiko , 1986-1987

Don't worry rabbit –
You'll find someone.

XXII
Yosei Harpyia

Butterfly with hand
clutches neck of winged woman
causing breast
to come out.

XXIII
Engoku, 1990-93

Crying girl
permanently
wears tears.

XXIV
Kogarashi no Yobigoe

Girl dressed in
invisible green
hugs herself to
make taller
tree woman
jealous
in the wind.

XXV
Party Night

Hand from off screen
surprises party girl

XXVI
Inochi

Girl with bullets
rifle
and carousel.
Snow globe.

XXVII
Hikari no Naka E
Tone!, 1991

Let's attack from the sun
in this horse
with this sword!

XXVIII
I would say I am still working on starting new revolutions.
~ Keiko Takemiya

XXIX
After a Takemiya drawing I don't remember the name of:

Well next time don't impale her with a spear
if you're going to get all sad about it.

XXX
Chibei no Yoake, 1984-85

You don't need a chair
in space.

Some of the other nearby drawings
indicate you also might not need pants
in space.

XXXI
Keith Anyan, 1977-80

Also known as the
Japanese Han Solo.

XXXII
Toi Hoshi no Kioku, 1977-80

She's been living inside my
head this whole time.

XXXIII
The main feature of the *Story Show*
1:30 pm showing was the story teller's
periodic maniacal laughter as she
changed story panels, and
encouraged us to join in.
I think I was made for this and
now I need to learn how to laugh
in Japanese.

XXXIV
The exhibition of past exhibit posters
is in the ceiling so they really mean it
when they say to look up to see it.

XXXV
Free manga grasshopper fans
for everyone!

XXXVI
Much of the museum is rooms and rooms of
The Wall of Manga with hundreds of
people sitting in chairs reading.
There is also the barefoot reading room
where they caution you may get
splinters in your feet.

Imperial Palace Grounds

When we enter the Imperial Palace Grounds
Addie immediately begins looking for
Imperial Bathrooms.

She spots familiar leaves and
asks if we should take some for dinner.
I wonder if whatever restaurant we're
going to will have a leafage fee.

Our itinerary changes when I decide
to go look at the imperial cat. She and
her friend want nothing to do with me.

Reading the history of the palace
we learn it was destroyed by fire
and reconstructed. Are there no old buildings
which haven't burned to the ground
only to present restorations to
generations of visitors
longing for the past?

I dream of being allowed to wait
in the Tiger room.

This is where we will dine tonight!
I say in my fancy voice,
outside *shishinden*.

My fly keeps coming down.
I'm fairly sure this is happening
on its own power

We can't view the imperial thrones
as they were transported to the Tokyo
Imperial Palace. Oh where oh where will
my imperial hiney dine tonight?

A sign under a bridge says
Mind your head.
It's not an issue, your majesty
as we walk on through.

We see the thick tatami mat
where the emperor sat and slept
and did all the imperial things
he needed to do.

The Pillow Book
by Sei Shōnagon —
A poet during
the time of this palace.
Poets have always been essential here.

We see a bridge
(a Japanese one of course)
we are not allowed to cross
even though we have come to it.

I think one of the palace security
guards is following me because of my
generally suspicious looking nature.
I have learned to sense when someone is
following me thanks to the many television
shows and movies about spies where they
invariably say *someone's tailing us.*
Also, while typing this, I think I lost her
which is also a skill I learned from
those same programs and movies when
they report back to someone on a
communication device that they
have lost them.

Poetry gatherings happened in
the Ogakumonjo building. Poetry rarely
comes to palaces any more.

They're teasing us with these beautiful
gardens stone pathways and, stone and
wooden bridges over running streams and
serene pools, and many ropes
preventing us from touching any of them
with our feet.

A thousand years —
this place was the seat of power
in Edo.

I'm trying hard not to fall down any stairs today.

That's really all I wanted to say.

Subway

I
We're heading to a bento box store
for everything you can imagine in
little mini (yes *little* and *mini*) compartments.
Addie has been training for this
her entire life.

II
Subways have refuge areas
in case you fall onto the tracks
and need somewhere to run
if a train is coming. I try not to
fall onto the tracks while taking
a picture of the sign explaining this
(as much as I want to see a refuge area.)

III
The handle
to hold onto
is too high.
I ask Addie
if she wants to
hold on to my face.
She declines.

Downfall

I've seen a single piece of trash
on the ground since we've arrived.
Today – just a minute ago. A fan.
The empire is crumbling.

In Front of the Otter Store

I
If I want, I can go into a store
in Teramachi Arcade where I
can pay money to touch the
hand of an otter. I get to look
at the otter too.

II
Warning in front of the store:
Since otters has chewing power,
you may get injured by play-bitting.

Gion Festival

Again, if you're missing any people odds are they are here.

At Koé Donuts

Our entertainment for the evening is
watching the *behind the scenes* action
at Koé Donuts.

Sitting near the *float factory* gives us
the perfect view of donuts being topped,
giant whisks in action, and the float factory itself

emptying of oil so someone can clean it.
Bye bye oil I say as it drains away.
The people next to us have ordered

from the premium menu and their
donuts are sliced and filled and
topped even more. The coffee cups

even at 8:30 at night, are attractively
Kong sized and I try to get Addie to
negotiate a sip for me while I step away.

Nothing has happened when I return
but the oil is already coming back
like Father New Year's children –

ready to live their whole lives.
*Welcome back oil. This is your
world now.*

End Feeling

Like today
this is all winding down.
A million people (no exaggeration)

in the streets
for the Gion Festival
A million steps (yes exaggeration)

on the device for the day.
Donuts, check.
Kimono sightings,

check check check!
We're calculating train rides
to the west.

We're strategizing
quick food. We're going to
Peace City tomorrow

Where a war ended
(like this evening ended)
when the ultimate in

humanity's ugliness
was displayed. This
will be almost the

last Japanese taste
in our mouths, or
on our tongues.

Whichever
you
prefer.

HIROSHIMA, THERE AND BACK

広島

What to Wear to the City of Peace

I'm running out of t-shirts
The red one that says *1776*
didn't seem right for Hiroshima.

The Led Zeppelin shirt was
too tight for this humidity and
the image of the Zeppelin crashing

was not for this. *Star Wars*
was left, which seemed benign
enough except the word

Wars felt wrong since
I'm traveling to the city of peace
forged by one of the many

wars that was meant
to end all wars.

An Ant on the Train to Kyoto Station

Is this where it lives
or does it commute to where
the breadcrumbs are?

More on This

Every bathroom in Japan displays
instructions on how to use the toilet.
Even on the bullet trains.
The only text I've seen in an
American bathroom is
We aim to please
so please aim.

poem

Today the racist who
runs my country

told people,
elected officials,

to go back to where
they came from.

Today I go to Hiroshima
to apologize for

yet another thing.

Dessert for Breakfast

I'm having a dessert sandwich for breakfast –
Fluffy white bread with whipped cream and
some kind of jelly. This is what I dreamed of
as a child – dessert for every meal. Now I'd
rather have eggs and this situation is
the result of a translation app that doesn't
know all it claims to.

Mood

I'm tired of *my country*
I'm all for tradition and culture
but I want borders to go away.

It's Probably Not What I think

A sign on a food stand at a train station
we pass through advertises *bukake*.
I don't know what they're selling but
alright Japan!

P.S. Autocorrect wants to change *bukake*
to *by kale*.

On the Train

I
The conductor turns and bows
before exiting the car. This is the
least *fuck you* culture ever.

II
I want to take a video
of the Japanese countryside
from the train window, but
every time I lift up my camera
we enter another tunnel.
No one wants to see
ten hours of home movies
from inside a dark tunnel.

III
We're starting the day
on an island with a floating gate
as long as it hasn't
floated away.

On Another Train

I
On the train from Hiroshima
to Miyajimaguchi station
we're seated directly facing
another couple. I want to be
polite and talk with them but
they speak another language
so we're left communicating
with a series of eyebrow
gestures and awkward smiles.

II
Now the man across from us
is eating his own thumb. This
is why you should never
skip breakfast.

III
The ancestors of
these faces lived through
the bomb.

IV
The sun is everywhere today.
Mt. Fuji, 709 kilometers away
is laughing at me.

V
Now he's eating another finger.
Grow your own food and thrive!

JR Miyajima Ferry

I
What I think is avant-garde saxophone jazz
is really just the creaks of the bridge to
get on the ferry as it rocks in the water.

II
Don't drop your phone or
JR Pass into Hiroshima Bay.
If they are meant to go in,
throw them purposefully.
It should not be an accident.

III
Judaism on a Boat:
Therefore choose lifejackets.

On Miyajima Island

I
The announcement on the island
tells us the deer are wild. They are
herbivores but they may eat our possessions
such as tickets or souvenirs.
We're going to risk it
and pet them anyway.

II
Rickshaw drivers have legs
bigger than all of you
put together.

III
I'm now one of those
people who uses an um-
brella in the sun.

IV
Tourists band together to
hold each other's possessions
so deer won't eat them while
we pose for photos.

V
We arrive at the shrine at
low tide so instead of floating
on water, it just floats.

VI
The deer want you to pet them
They want your hands on their hands.
They don't care who you are –
Just if you're willing to give them attention
or put food in their mouths.
The squirrels back in Van Nuys
could learn a lot from these deer.

VII
Addie sees a group of deer
standing in front of a group of humans
and says *the deer are photo crashing*.
I tell her sometimes they call that *photo bombing*.
She smiles, well aware, saying she doesn't want
to use the word *bombing* in Hiroshima.

VIII
Momiji manjū
special to this Island
come in many flavors
and are kind of like
maple leaf shaped
souped up Twinkies.

Thought on the Ferry

I see a sign that says *hose box*.
I need a hose box like I need a
hose in the head.

Train to Where it Happened

I
There is no graffiti here
There are no people begging for
money or food. No one gets on
the train to tell you their sad story
between stops. This is Japan.
This is all of Japan.

II
I give up my seat for
a woman who needs a seat.
I have no business taking
anything from anyone
in this city.

III
We are two tram stops away
from ground zero.

Hiroshima

*I will forever dream, simply as I did in my boyhood,
and therefore suffer little.*
   ~Miekichi Suzuki

In the Peace Park

It destroyed a neighborhood to start.
The first used on humankind.

They leave Genbaku Dome as it was.
Ruins shall be preserved forever.

The joy that must have happened in this dome
before August 6, 1945

Hiroshima Prefectural Commercial Exhibition Hall

This place is a *Yad Vashem*.
Yad Vashem is a Peace Dome.

Sadako Sasaki, bombed at two
Leukemia death at ten

*This is our cry, this is our prayer
for building peace in this world*

A thousand
paper cranes

There is no playground in this park
where children used to play.

Museum

A group of Japanese visitors
seems a little too giddy
on the elevator to the
permanent exhibition.

Hiroshima before the bombing
was an *alive* place
Then, skeletons of trees

It took seconds.
One hundred forty thousand dead
by the end of 1945.

No more Hiroshimas

Another half-crazed mother cradled her small child,
calling its name repeatedly and crying,
"Open your eyes! Open your eyes!"

Sheets of burnt skin
hung from them like rags.

Soon the fires spread over the entire city
filling the sky with gray smoke.

It was deep-red,
perhaps a sort of blackish orange.
A vivid intense color
I'd never seen before.

A huge cloud of smoke
Like nothing I'd seen before.

The city was instantly destroyed
Many people were killed, not knowing
what had happened to them.
A chimney that didn't collapse
From on top of a soy sauce factory
The names of grave stones burned away

Everything is measured by
number of meters from the hypocenter.

Students with their skins burned off
A *Holocaust* in an instant
Corpses turned red blue and purple
Corpses floating in the river
A human shadow etched in stone

Black rain
Radioactive rain
Thirsty woman catching
black rain in mouth

Relief began on the day of —
People transported to the suburbs

Cries of the soul —
My hair is falling out.
How could this have happened to me
It hurts it hurts!
I don't want to die.
I'm sorry I cannot save you.

A mother collected ashes
from several places but
could confirm none as
her fourteen year old son
Hajime Fukuoka.

Please give this to my family on Miyajima Island.
         ~Kazuo Kojima (15)

So terrible to lose a smart young man like him.

The atomic bomb destroyed lives
without regard to national or ethnic origins.

They had to go on with their lives.

Many of the elderly – left behind
robbed of their will to live.

Children who lost their parents
Parents who lost their children

Where shall I bury the body
of my dead child?

Deep scars on
minds and bodies

Children in wombs
exposed to radiation

They nicknamed the bomb
Little Boy

Counting money daily –
It was never enough.

Unbearable pain

The rest of their lives
They carried pain that
never went away.

On the night of August 6
the moon was as bright as ever.

To live as long as life lasts
fold a thousand cranes

fold them for Sadako.
No more Hiroshimas.

Never again.

School children laughing
and enjoying each other
in the lobby after the museum.

At Hiroshima Station

I
You can get frozen okonomiyaki
at the Eikie Food Market in case you were
enchanted by what you had in the restaurant
and want to make it at home.

II
We learn the limits of the JR Passes
when they tell us we can't ride the
Nozomi trains to Shin-Osaka, and
spend an extra hour in Hiroshima station
tasting things we thought were sugar
coated lychee, but which turned out to be
sugar coated grapes.

Here's what you need to know about your trip to Japan:

You have not allotted enough time for your trip.
You have not allotted enough time in each city on your trip.
You have not allotted enough time for each neighborhood you visit.

Japan takes forever and if you planned to travel here forever
you would still not have enough time to see it all.

Plan an extra hour, an extra day, an extra week, an extra year.
Tell your boss you'll be back when you've worshipped at every shrine.
Ask her if she likes lychee. Tell her it was the honor of your life
to have worked for her. Clap twice. Bow.

You still do not have enough time.

Still At Hiroshima Station

I
A man in the waiting room
moves so two vacant seats can
accommodate Addie and me.
Later he moved again to
accommodate the same thing
for two other people.
His job is to move from one seat
to another to allow pairs of people
to sit together.

II
An unnecessary ringing noise happens
in the Shinkansen waiting area, enclosed
in glass for our comfort, but allowing the ringing
to ring louder. *Let's torture the waiters with this
ringing noise*, someone thought up at
a meeting one day, and now the noise
gets louder as if it knows I'm thinking about it.
Rather than scream in protest, I decide to join in
like a native war cry – Native to where
I don't know. Here comes the noise again.
Lalalallalalallalalalallalalalalalallalalal.
(I'm trilling.)

Train Back

I
The lady who does the voice on the train
is the same lady who does the voice in
the elevator at our hotel, and in the elevator
at the Gion subway station. She does get
around, but mostly I'm just thrilled that
elevators keep talking to me.

II
The big question now is
when we get back to Kyoto
do we want to wait in line
for an hour to get *something*
on a stick.

III
Nighttime Japan goes
by through Shinkansen window.
Bullets heading east.

IV
I wonder if there are a lot of people
with legs in Shin Osaka.

V
Do you remember,
earlier in this book,
when I would mention
The Tokyo-Van Nuys Express a lot?
Whatever happened to that?

VI
The moon is
as bright as ever
outside this train.

VII
The seat in front of us
is prominently rattling.
I want to join in with this
noise too, or add the
battle cry from the station
to create a harmony or
maybe the first ever
orchestra composed only
of trains and train stations.
(Addie wants none of this.)

VIII
The book you are reading
I am writing it right now.
This is what it's like
in the future. Or maybe
hello from the past!

In the Stick Line

Addie and I have returned to Gion
and have decided to stand in line
to get whatever it is that comes
on sticks. Neither of us are hungry.
Neither of us know what it is they
are putting on the sticks. No one
in the line speaks English. This is
our last chance to be in the stick line
This is our last chance to get whatever
is on the sticks.

Our plan is to buy a stick with things on it.
If it turns out to be fish, Addie will eat it.
If it's meat of some other kind, neither of
is will eat it. We're praying it's a dessert dough
drizzled with a sweet sauce – Maybe dumplings.
There's definitely a stick. Now Addie is thinking
it could be a savory dumpling. Time will tell.

A young Asian man just identified us in the line
and asked us (in English) what we were waiting for.
We told him we weren't sure and he walked away.
But the fact that he asked us proves the theory of
the magnetic draw of the line. This line to be specific.
We wouldn't get in any line. Though there is a
comfort to being a part of a system. Even if it takes
long stick line time.

Hello. What are we in line for
I'll ask the woman when she gets to us.

She asked me *how many?*
I asked her *how many come in it?*
She scolded me for asking *how many*
when it was her job to ask *how many*.

We ordered two.
Two of whatever they are.
Addie thinks they're wrapped in leaves.

Addie thinks it's ridiculous
we're standing in this line
and only ordering two.

Rule number one of the stick line is
don't ask what's on the stick.

Honestly at this point I'm not going
to tell you what was on the sticks.
All I'll say is now we're both

sticky.

My Across the Ocean Neighbor Totoro

It is early where you are.
Here in Japan it is late, but also tomorrow.
I'm sitting in the lobby of the hotel enjoying
the waning moments of my last night.
The Totoro theme (instrumental version)
is playing on the lobby speakers while
a Japanese Whiskey sits to my right.
Totoro may be a creature known as
a Koropokkuru from Shinto folklore.
For sure it is a forest creature with
an umbrella, and when he chooses
the largest smile this side of the Pacific.
We began this adventure on that side
of the Pacific...excited to be flying
this way for the first time. Our second
day brought us to Totoro. So how fitting
he should put the first piece of the
Tokyo-Van Nuys Express bookend
into place. We were in Hiroshima today.
We are in Kyoto today. We will be in
California tomorrow. These are the
possibilities of this world.

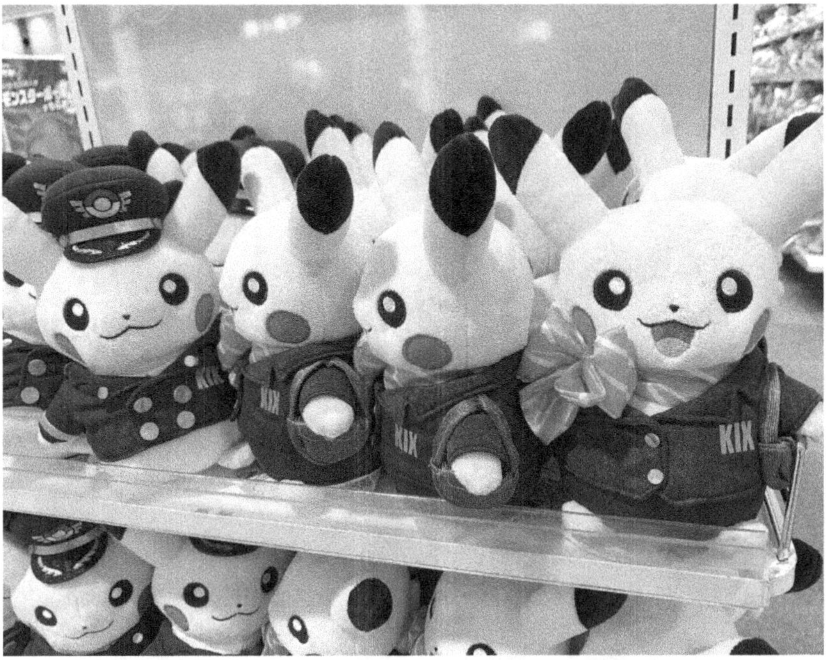

THE TOKYO-VAN NUYS EXPRESS HEADS TO VAN NUYS

宅

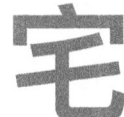

Last

I brushed my teeth for
the last time in Japan.
I took full advantage of
all the room amenities
since soon we'll be
fending for ourselves.

I walked to breakfast
for the last time in Japan.
Soon most breakfasts
will be down the Van Nuys hall.
Clapton was playing in
the restaurant. He's
from England but he
reminds me of home.

A roasted Japanese tea latte
with black honey is coming soon.
We're steps from our hotel
steps and steps from the train
that will take us away.

Clapton is singing about
the San Francisco Bay.
That's close enough for
our purposes.

They don't want children
in this restaurant, which
is fine as we don't have any
with us. We're going to
get one soon. A used model.
But we're okay with that as
we're the ones who've been
using him.

The trains under my feet
are calling our names.

Last Minute Shopping

I
We pass by *Paris Hair and Face*
which sells neither hair
nor faces.

II
Overheard in Gion:

A: I've got two bug bites.
R: Face it momma - you taste sweet!

III
Every matcha bowl is different.
If you find two that are the same
throw them both away.
Neither are legitimate.

IV
We're seeing many cute
things in the shops and
with each new thing
Addie's squeals of delight
are getting more and more
high pitched. There was a lot of
sugar at breakfast and an overload
is happening.

In Kyoto Station

People carrying nothing
turn into people carrying backpacks
turn into people wheeling luggage
as we get closer to the *Haruka* train
that will take us to the airport.

Hello Train

Our third of three trains to the airport is decorated with *Hello Kitty* on the inside and outside. Considering the nature of this point in time we'd like to rebrand her *Goodbye Kitty*.

Airport

I
The elevator woman voice
has showed up on the airport
escalator to bid us farewell.

II
Bidets in the Kansai Osaka Airport bathrooms?
You bet your sweet and immaculate hiney!

Semaphorically

The semaphore workers
stand outside the plane and

wave goodbye as we taxi away.
Both sides of the plane I hope.

They want people to hold on to
their babies during takeoff.

We take off.
Japan drifts away.

Plane

I
I'm watching a movie about
old people who rob banks.
I'm not being disrespectful.
Old man is in the title.

II
Fuji briefly visible
out my window. I knew
she wouldn't let me down.

III
We fly into night.
Yesterday is on
the horizon.

IV
I'm wearing my Zeppelin shirt.
It is comfortable and I am
going to California.

V
Green tea ice cream is coming.
I chose that flavor to keep
Japan going on my taste buds.

VI
I'm two movies into the
Pacific Ocean. Someone should
win an Oscar for all of this.

Somewhere Over the Pacific

I
Last night at this time
Addie reminds me
we were standing in
the stick line.

II
Bidet in the airplane bathroom?
You bet your high flyin' hiney!

III
California is outside the window –
Right where I left it.

IV
Japan Airlines branded shoehorn
to the rescue!

V
The flight path takes us over our house
and Jude's camp.

VI
405 freeway –
That's what I'm
talking about.

VII
Wheels down.

LAX

Customs
Over ten thousand dollars in cash?
In my dreams, officer!

Bidet in LAX Bathroom?
Not a chance.
This vacation is over!

There and Here

It is already tomorrow back in Japan.
It is still yesterday here in Los Angeles
in so many ways.

THE JAPANESE WORD FOR DENOUEMENT WHICH IS A FRENCH WORD

終局

Quiet

It is never this quiet in our house.
Addie is buying groceries and Jude,
for all I know, is on a horse.

I know for sure I've got a few more days
without aggravated remote control clicking,
without yelling at people over a headset.

In Japan, children are not allowed to
make noise until they are thirty five.
I made that up but this is

creative writing and I'm feeling creative.
We had homemade Japanese dinner
tonight, homemade with Addie's hands

and the things she found at the stores
and our recent memories of small portions
served one at a time so no items

felt crowded by any others and, as one
menu said, portions were *perfectly sized*.
It's all over on Sunday. We drive back

to the Simi Valley to pick up our
favorite noise. We've got a hose ready.
A pair of scissors. We expect we'll

need a second car for his fingernails.
I'll miss the quiet but I know it'll be just
a handful of fast moving years before

the quiet doesn't go away.
It goes so fast they say.
It is going so fast.

I miss the Japanese shower water pressure

but not the Japanese hotel hair dryers
with their so-called "turbo" mode.

Youth

Everyone in Japan is young
except for the old people

but you don't see many of them.
I saw a man driving a boat

outside of Kyoto who might
have been old but he wouldn't say.

Everyone in Japan is young
But don't tell them I said that.

I'm Still Writing This Book

Addie wants to know how long
this book is going to be since it's
three days after we've returned
from Japan and I'm still writing it.
Pretty long I tell her. We're in
a long line of cars to get into
the camp where we left our
ten year old three weeks ago
and, as far as I'm concerned,
it's still vacation until he's
hosed down, and the never-ending
cycle of washing his clothes
starts up again. We've packed him
in the car now. We're going to
get eggs before we take him home.
See if we can't make this last
just a little longer.

Goodbye

The Tokyo-Van Nuys Express has reached its final stop. Please disembark and continue on with the rest of your life.

ABOUT THE AUTHOR

The author, getting the hang of how to pose for pictures in Japan

Three-time Pushcart Prize, and Best of the Net nominee Rick Lupert has been involved with poetry in Los Angeles since 1990. He was awarded the Beyond Baroque Distinguished Service Award in 2014 for service to the Los Angeles poetry community. He served for two years as a co-director of the non-profit literary organization Valley Contemporary Poets. His poetry has appeared in numerous magazines and literary journals, including *The Los Angeles Times, Rattle, Chiron Review, Red Fez, Zuzu's Petals, Stirring, The Bicycle Review, Caffeine Magazine, Blue Satellite* and others. He edited the anthologies *A Poet's Siddur: Shabbat Evening - Liturgy Through the Eyes of Poets, Ekphrastia Gone Wild - Poems Inspired by Art, A Poet's Haggadah: Passover through the Eyes of Poets,* and *The Night Goes on All Night - Noir Inspired Poetry,* and is the author of twenty-four other books: *Hunka Hunka Howdee!, 17 Holy Syllables, God Wrestler: A Poem for Every Torah Portion,* (Ain't Got No Press) *Beautiful Mistakes, Donut Famine, Romancing the Blarney Stone, Professor Clown on Parade, Making Love to the 50 Ft. Woman, The Gettysburg Undress* (Rothco Press), *Nothing in New England is New, Death of a Mauve Bat, Sinzibuckwud!, We Put Things In Our Mouths, Paris: It's The Cheese, I Am My Own Orange County, Mowing Fargo, I'm a Jew. Are You?, Feeding Holy Cats, Stolen Mummies, I'd Like to Bake Your Goods, A Man With No Teeth Serves Us Breakfast* (Ain't Got No Press), *Lizard King of the Laundromat, Brendan Constantine is My Kind of Town* (Inevitable Press) and *Up Liberty's Skirt* (Cassowary Press), and the spoken word album *Rick Lupert Live and Dead* (Ain't Got No Press). He hosted the long running Cobalt Café reading series in Canoga Park for almost twenty-one years, relaunched in 2020 as a virtual series, and has read his poetry all over the world.

Rick created *Poetry Super Highway*, an online resource and publication for poets (PoetrySuperHighway.com), *Haikuniverse*, a daily online small poem publication (Haikuniverse.com), and writes and occasionally draws the daily web comic *Cat and Banana* with Brendan Constantine. (facebook.com/catandbanana) He also writes the weekly Jewish poetry blog *From the Lupertverse* for JewishJournal.com

Rick works as a music teacher at synagogues in Southern California and as a graphic and web designer for anyone who would like to help pay his mortgage.

RICK'S OTHER BOOKS AND RECORDINGS

Hunka Hunka Howdee!
Ain't Got No Press ~ May, 2019

Beautiful Mistakes
Rothco Press ~ May, 2018

17 Holy Syllables
Ain't Got No Press ~ January, 2018

A Poet's Siddur: Friday Evening (edited by)
Ain't Got No Press ~ November, 2017

God Wrestler: A Poem for Every Torah Portion
Ain't Got No Press ~ August, 2017

Donut Famine
Rothco Press ~ December, 2016

Romancing the Blarney Stone
Rothco Press ~ December, 2016

Professor Clown on Parade
Rothco Press ~ December, 2016

Rick Lupert Live and Dead (Album)
Ain't Got No Press ~ March, 2016

Making Love to the 50 Ft. Woman
Rothco Press ~ May, 2015

The Gettysburg Undress
Rothco Press ~ May, 2014

Ekphrastia Gone Wild (edited by)
Ain't Got No Press ~ July, 2013

Nothing in New England is New
Ain't Got No Press ~ March, 2013

Death of a Mauve Bat
Ain't Got No Press ~ January, 2012

The Night Goes On All Night Noir Inspired Poetry (edited by)
Ain't Got No Press ~ November, 2011

Sinzibuckwud!
Ain't Got No Press ~ January, 2011

We Put Things In Our Mouths
Ain't Got No Press ~ January, 2010

 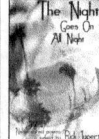  

A Poet's Haggadah (edited by)
Ain't Got No Press ~ April, 2008

A Man With No Teeth Serves Us Breakfast
Ain't Got No Press ~ May, 2007

I'd Like to Bake Your Goods
Ain't Got No Press ~ January, 2006

Stolen Mummies
Ain't Got No Press ~ February, 2003

Brendan Constantine is My Kind of Town
Inevitable Press ~ September, 2001

Up Liberty's Skirt
Cassowary Press ~ March, 2001

Feeding Holy Cats
Cassowary Press ~ May, 2000

I'm a Jew, Are You?
Cassowary Press ~ May, 2000

Mowing Fargo
Sacred Beverage Press ~ December, 1998

Lizard King of the Laundromat
The Inevitable Press ~ February, 1998

I Am My Own Orange County
Ain't Got No Press ~ May, 1997

Paris: It's The Cheese
Ain't Got No Press ~ May, 1996

For more information:
www.PoetrySuperHighway.com

www.ingramcontent.com/pod-product-compliance
Lightning Source LLC
Chambersburg PA
CBHW071335080526
44587CB00017B/2846